GEORGE BEST
with ROSS BENSON

THE GOOD,
THE BAD AND
THE BUBBLY

SIMON & SCHUSTER

LONDON·SYDNEY·NEW YORK·TOKYO·SINGAPORE·TORONTO

First published in Great Britain by
Simon & Schuster Ltd in 1990
A Paramount Communications Company

Copyright © George Best and Ross Benson, 1990

Simon & Schuster Ltd
West Garden Place
Kendal Street
London W2 2AQ

Simon & Schuster of Australia Pty Ltd
Sydney

A CIP catalogue record for this book is
available from the British Library
ISBN 0–671–71026–5

Typeset in Trump Medieval 11/13
by Falcon Typographic Art Ltd
Printed and bound in Great Britain by
Billing & Sons Ltd, Worcester

Contents

Prologue

I PUNCHED MICHAEL Caine to the floor in Tramp one night. I punched Tim Jeffries, the former husband of Prince Andrew's ex-girlfriend, Koo Stark, to the floor in Tramp another night. I am now banned from Tramp. After the Jeffries incident Johnny Gold, the owner, said to me, 'George, enough is enough – that's it.' He had a point.

Tramp, built in a basement in Jermyn Street in the St. James's area of central London, is one of the smartest, most fashionable discotheques in the world. Dark lights, loud music, smart men, beautiful women. On your left as you come down the stairs is the dance floor. On the right there is an elegant, dimly lit restaurant which sells vintage champagne and sausage and mash arranged on the plate to resemble the male genitals. The Duchess of York goes there. So do most of the world's top pop stars and film actors. They go there to eat and drink and dance and let their hair down. They don't go there to become embroiled in fights.

I used to go there a lot. It's a private club with a lot of famous members. No one asks you for an autograph in Tramp. No one bothers you, which is why I liked it so much. I could relax there. I would go there, sometimes by myself, usually with a girlfriend, and enjoy a quiet bottle of wine or champagne in a corner. And that's the way I like it. I'm not a fighting drunk. If I never had another fight in my life that would be fine by me. I very rarely had fights when I was a boy; I don't like having fights now. But I don't like being insulted, and it was his barrage of offensive remarks that led me into my fracas with Caine.

I walked in with Mary Stavin, the former Miss World who was my girlfriend at the time. It was a relationship of mutual convenience. I was using her and she was using me; there was never any strong affection between us, at least, not from me. That, however, is not the explanation for what happened next.

1

Michael was sitting at Johnny Gold's table just to the right of the doorway in the restaurant. Johnny invited us to join them. I think Michael was slightly the worse for wear and I was not too far behind him. I might even have been in front of him. At first everything was fine. I introduced Michael to Mary for the fifteenth time – when Michael is under the weather he has severe memory lapses. Michael was very chatty, and somewhere along the way he said to Mary how beautiful she was and how he could understand her being Miss World and how his wife, Shakira, had finished third in the Miss World contest a few years before. As a joke I said, 'Michael, you're such a crawler.'

Caine went mad. He asked me who I thought I was talking to. He suggested I perform several anatomical impossibilities and went on to ask, 'Why don't you and your bird get the hell out of here?'

Poor Johnny was stuck in the middle between us and he didn't know quite what to do. Nor did I. I thought Caine was joking. I started to laugh, but Caine wasn't letting go. He asked me what I was laughing at. I said, 'You are joking, aren't you Mike?'

He said he wasn't, and asked me: 'Why don't you bugger off and go and drink somewhere else?'

Still Johnny hadn't said a word. He's known us both for years and I suppose that, like me, he thought Caine was going to start laughing any second and say that he was just having a bit of fun. But he didn't and by now Mary was getting very embarrassed. She nudged me and said, 'Come on, let's get out of here.'

I said, 'Michael, I think you should apologise to Mary.' He didn't. He kept snarling and growling and telling us to leave. After a few more moments of this I said to Mary, 'Come on, we're going.' We stood up. We made it to the doorway of the restaurant which leads into the lounge area and the stairs leading out. Then I lost my temper. I thought, 'Why should I leave? Why should I put up with that kind of behaviour?' I said to Mary, 'Hang on a moment, I'm going back.'

I went over to the table and said, 'Mike, I'm going to give you one more chance to apologise and if you don't I'm going to smack you.' I got the predictable reply. Then he started to get up off his chair. As he did so I hit him.

2

It wasn't so much a punch as a slap but it sent him flying backwards off his chair. He ended up on his backside on the floor with his glasses hanging off his nose. It was like a sketch from the old Morecambe and Wise show.

The waiters came running over shouting, 'Oh please, Mr George,' 'Please, Señor Best.' I then turned on Johnny and told him I thought he was out of order, that I hadn't done anything wrong, that we had been friends for over 20 years, that he should have intervened when Caine started insulting Mary and me. It wasn't Johnny's fault, of course. He just happened to get caught in the crossfire.

The good thing was that I wasn't really drunk. If I had been the situation might have got completely out of hand. As it was relations were rather strained for a while, but in those days everybody was always bumping into everyone else and I kept seeing Michael – at parties and premières and at lunch at Langan's restaurant in Mayfair which Michael part-owned and where I sometimes ate – and eventually we got together, admitted we were both a little drunk at the time and agreed to forget it. His explanation did make me laugh, though. He said that he had had a few drinks because he was having problems on *The Jigsaw Man*, the film he was working on at the time.

I said, 'Michael, don't tell me about your problems. I'm in the middle of a divorce. I'm being made bankrupt. I'm being treated for alcoholism. Those are my problems. You get paid a million dollars for yours.'

And that was it. We shook hands and we have been okay with each other since.

There was no such happy ending to the Tim Jeffries incident, however. I was going out with Angie Lynn at the time and we'd split up again for the umpteenth time. I was in a bad way. I was completely infatuated with Angie and I missed her. I was drinking heavily and by the time I got to Tramp that particular evening I was very drunk.

I had heard, wrongly as it turned out, that Angie was getting into drugs. That upset me. I don't take drugs and I knew that Angela couldn't afford them. My drink-sodden mind started putting two and two together and coming up with a multiplication of wrong answers. I figured that if she was taking drugs then whoever she was with must be supplying them to her.

Angie was sitting next to Johnny's table, the same table at which I had hit Caine. I can't remember if I spoke a word to Angela. I do remember saying to the girl I was with that I wanted to get out of there because I knew there was going to be trouble if I stayed.

We walked around the corner to another discotheque called Xenon. The girl I was with went to the bathroom, and like a fool I left her in there and walked back to Tramp. I went in, walked down the stairs, turned right through the ante-room into the restaurant and went over to Angela. She says I grabbed her. I say I didn't. To be honest I can't remember one way or the other.

The next thing I knew someone had jumped on my back. I started fighting back and the two of us ended up rolling around on the floor with people around us screaming and scattering. It turned out I was fighting with Tim Jeffries who had just started taking Angie out. I didn't know who Tim Jeffries was – I didn't find out until afterwards – and if I passed him in the street tomorrow I wouldn't recognise him. But it didn't matter; that night I would have fought with anyone.

Once again the waiters came rushing over. This time they were not so polite. They grabbed me and bundled me up the stairs, kicking and shouting and swearing, and out into the street. That was the last time I was in Tramp. A few days later Johnny sent me a typewritten letter saying that I was no longer welcome in the club. I was totally out of order. I should never have behaved the way I did but I just couldn't help myself. I snapped. I regret the whole episode – and the fact that it happened to be Johnny's birthday dinner certainly didn't help matters.

That's the way it has been these past years. Fights, women, drink, walk-outs, walk-backs, sometimes the villain, sometimes the victim – and always news whether I liked it or not.

It's a long way from the Cregagh estate in Belfast.

Chapter One

Early Days

I WAS BORN on 22 May 1946 into a solid, working-class family, Protestant by religion, decent and honest in its beliefs.

My father, Dick, was an iron turner at the Harland and Wolff shipyard. My mother, Ann, worked part-time to bring in extra money. They were a typical hard-working couple doing their best for their family.

Belfast was a better place to live in those days. The troubles had not started and on the Cregagh, the vast, sprawling council estate where I was brought up, Catholic and Protestant lived side by side and no one gave much thought to that. To my adult eye the Cregagh looks grey and soulless but it did not seem like that when I was a youngster. There was no broken glass on the roads or graffiti paint-gunned on the walls of the houses. Then it was home and I had a happy childhood there, and the memories I carry with me – of boyhood scrapes and family Sundays and Saturday matinées at the cinema and outings with my parents – are pleasant ones. I was popular and I had a lot of friends, more friends than most. I enjoyed school, I was good at my lessons and I was very good at sport.

Like all boys I had my dreams. If I was not pretending to be Zorro I was dreaming of being a famous football player. I knew I was good. I knew I was a better player than the other boys, and I would imagine myself scoring the winning goal for Wolverhampton Wanderers, the team I supported as a boy, in the F.A. Cup final at Wembley. I never did play for Wolves. To my great regret I never played in the F.A. Cup final. And by the time I reached my teens I had almost given up any idea of becoming a professional footballer. It was one thing to fantasise in a boyish way about something. It's quite another thing to achieve it and because of my size – I was very skinny, with arms so thin they embarrassed me – I had more or less resigned myself to becoming the printer my father wanted me to be.

He suggested that would be a good trade to be in because there would always be a job there and unemployment was always a concern on the Cregagh. He could still remember the post-war years, and so could I, when rationing was still in force, an apple was a treat, a banana was a luxury and life was a dour struggle. But at least most of the people on our estate were in work and folk from some other parts of the city used to refer to us as the well-off snobs. That was nonsense. All the families we knew were hard-working. A lot of them were struggling. Some of them had big families; there was a Catholic woman who lived down the street from us who had 14 children and keeping them all clothed and fed was obviously not easy. Everybody managed to get by, however, and whatever problems there may have been elsewhere in Belfast everyone on the Cregagh mixed in.

We very rarely locked our doors. In those days you didn't have to and even today, when I go home to see my father who still lives in the same house I lived in when I was a little boy, I have to shout after him to remind him to shut the front door when he goes out of the house. People were always coming and going into each other's houses and because it was a new estate, full of young families, there were children everywhere, playing in the street, popping in for cups of tea or glasses of lemonade, asking if Jimmy or Johnny or George could come out to play.

I got into all the usual scrapes. I was a bit of a nutcase, I suppose. I was always trying to do things people said you couldn't do and I was always getting bruised for my efforts. Down at the bottom of our street is a river with one bank higher than the other. All the children used to jump from the high bank down onto the low one. I was the one, of course, who decided I was going to leap the other way. Nobody had ever attempted that before and halfway across I found out why.

I took a running jump at it, lifted off, got part of the way over, realised that I wasn't going to make it and ended up almost impaling myself on a piece of metal sticking out of the concrete bank. It caught me between my legs. The pain was excruciating and one part of my life was almost ended

Blissful innocence. Outside the house in Belfast, aged a few months.

even before it had begun. I didn't cry, not until I'd hobbled home and had safely locked myself in the bathroom. I didn't want anyone to see me cry. But I could never be persuaded to try it again.

I wasn't very keen on playing goalkeeper either. The first time (and just about the last time) I played in goal I dislocated a finger on my right hand. Someone kicked the ball. I tried to stop it. The ball caught my finger and snapped it back.

It was the middle of the afternoon, but my father was at home. He was working on a night shift and he was in bed asleep. I woke him up waving my hanging finger under his nose. It was quite a simple injury. My father took me to the hospital and the doctor clicked it back into place straight away. If I'd known how to do it I could have done it myself and I did, when I dislocated it again years later during a game at Old Trafford.

In those days, however, hospitals were something of a habit with me. I never wore slippers around the house, despite my mother's pestering. One day she broke a milk bottle on the kitchen floor. We cleaned up the mess and hunted around for the last sliver. I found it. I stood on it and it embedded itself in my foot. My father took me to the hospital. The nurse, an old battle-axe, poked around with a needle. At one stage I jumped. She said, in a heavy, officious voice, 'You keep still.' My father got angry at that. 'He's only a boy – don't speak to him like that.'

I was convinced that the piece of glass was still there. The nurse wasn't. She said there was nothing wrong with me and sent me away. About a month later I was running home from school. As I came down the path I felt a pain in my foot. I took my shoe off and found a piece of glass which had finally worked its way out. It was about an inch long. I kept it and showed it to my father when he came home from work. He was furious. He went straight to the hospital, looking for the nurse. I don't think he found her, which is just as well. That, though, is the way my father was. He was very protective of his family, very supportive, and that is no bad father for a boy to have. He provided a sense of security and he made me feel safe.

There was a boy who lived down the street named John Huntsdale, as I recall, and he was regarded as something of a bully. My friends and I had a meeting and decided that one of us was going to have to sort him out. We drew lots and I got the job because, I suppose, I was a little crazier than the rest, though oddly enough this was the only real fight I remember having as a child.

We met at the end of the road on a patch of bare ground where the Protestants used to hold their bonfires on the night before the Orangemen's March on 12 July, and I was not looking forward to it. I was only about 11 and a skinny little kid. He was two or three years older and he seemed two or three feet taller.

The other children formed a circle around us and we went to it. There was a lot of shouting and cheering, a lot of, 'Come on George, hit him.' There was nothing to it at the start, just a lot of pushing and posturing. It was like we were slapping each other with handbags. Then he started hurting me and I got angry. We were rolling round on the waste ground the way boys do. I saw a piece of glass and I rubbed his arm on it. I slashed it open and blood started running. That was the end of the fight. He started crying, everyone drifted away into the shadows; I panicked and ran home.

Two days later the boy's father came knocking at our front door. I was upstairs but I knew who it was; I'd been waiting, the way children do, for something like this to happen. My father opened the door. I was peering down the staircase and I could hear my father say, 'Can I help you?'

'Yes,' the man said. 'Your son beat my son up a couple of days ago. What are you going to do about it?'

My father replied, 'What are you talking about, "beat him up"? You're Mr Huntsdale with a son who is six feet tall and you're telling me that my little fellow has beaten your son up?'

He said, 'Yes, and I want you to do something about it.'

I was frightened. I thought, oh dear, this is it. Then my father said, 'Get out of here. Don't ever come round annoying my family or I'll sort you out.'

My father became something of a hero to me after that. That was his way – open, outfront, always prepared to stand up for his side. He had played amateur football for a local team when he was younger, and though I never actually saw him play, friends of his tell me that he was a very pugnacious player, always getting stuck in.

He wasn't the real athlete in the family, though. That was my mother. During the week she worked. I rarely saw her during the day and I usually had to get my own lunch and tea, which isn't as deprived as it sounds. A lot of the mothers on the estate had jobs and my mother worked in a fish and chip shop and then for a while in an ice-cream factory, and I used to pop in to see her and get the left-over chips or ice lollipops. At the weekend she played hockey and she was very good. I used to go and watch her and, in my memory at least, she scored at least once every game. She was quick, sharp and aggressive.

Off the field she was a very different character, however. She was very quiet and only rarely lost her temper. If I was naughty she would occasionally clip me across the back of the legs with her hand but she told me later, when I was older, how she hated doing that. She was not just being sensitive – because I was so skinny it used to hurt her hand more than it hurt me. I would roll up into a little ball on the floor and she would be hitting bone more than flesh.

That didn't happen very often. On the whole I was a well mannered and reasonably behaved child. I went through a brief stage of shoplifting, but only for stamps. I'd started collecting them and to add to my collection I started nicking them from the counter at Woolworths. I would pick up half a dozen packets, drop them on the floor, pick them up, only put five back on the counter, and walk quickly out of the shop with the sixth one hidden under my coat. It was hardly organised crime and I only did it a few times. I never got caught and if I had I'm certain my mother would have given me a good thrashing. As it was she spent most of her time sticking plasters onto grazed knees rather than slapping the back of them.

There was the Zorro incident. Saturday afternoons it was the children's matinée at the local cinema and all the kids from the Cregagh used to go. The admission was either a few pennies or an empty jam jar. There was a glass shortage in Belfast at the time and if you took along an empty jam jar you got in free. If you didn't have a jam jar you sent a friend in to open the side door. Very few people actually paid money to get in.

We used to have events like yo-yo competitions on the stage, but it was the films we were there to see. The Lone Ranger, Hopalong Cassidy and, our favourite, Zorro. We all liked Zorro and afterwards we would fasten our school gabardine coats like a cape and run home pretending to have sword fights.

On my way into the theatre one afternoon I tripped on a hole in the floor and caught my head on one of the metal-sided seats. I could feel the blood but I didn't bother about it and just kept patting my head with my handkerchief. When I got home my mother took one look at me and screamed. The whole of one side of my face was caked in blood. I looked like a crash victim. 'Why didn't you come home?' she wanted to know.

I explained that I couldn't leave, not in the middle of Zorro, not when the masked avenger was galloping across the screen.

Just before I sat my 11-plus I posed (seated second from left) with my classmates from Nettlefield Primary School. I was the only one who passed the exam.

'You silly bugger,' she said and I was off down the hospital again to have stitches put into the long, deep gash I'd collected above my eye.

My childhood wasn't all blood and injury, of course. We were a close family and whenever we got the chance my father and I would go off on long bicycle rides together. We would cycle, 15, 20 miles out of Belfast and down to the seaside to collect little shellfish we called willets which we brought home and cooked in a big pot. My father was the only one who ate them. Everybody else hated them, particularly my mother; they stank the house out for a week afterwards. She much preferred our outings to the seaside town of Bangor.

It was only a few miles down the coast but in those days it seemed like we were going to the other side of the world. We would take a train in the morning, myself, my mother and father, and later, my sisters Carol and Barbara. The routine was always the same. When we got off the train my mother went straight into the bingo hall. My father and I would leave her there and go off and have some ice-cream and then play a

11

couple of rounds on the putting green before wandering back to join her.

She loved playing bingo in that big, old-fashioned hall. I would sit on one side of her, my father would sit on the other, and we would all join in. They didn't draw numbers out of a hat there. Instead a man pulling a wheeled container with all the numbers displayed in different colours would come round and hand you a ball which you had to throw onto the number you wanted. I never managed to hit the right number but my mother did and she would spend hours in there. When we finally managed to get her out we would go round to the fish and chip shop, then stroll around the arcades and spend a few pennies on the slot machines before catching a train back to the city.

We did that for years and years and if things hadn't worked out the way they did I'd probably still be doing it now.

We were quite a religious family and Sunday was the only day of the week when I didn't go out to kick a football around. We always spent the Sabbath with my grandparents, with my mother's parents, who we had lived with until we moved the few miles up the road to the Cregagh estate when I was two. The whole family gathered – cousins, uncles, aunts – and we spent the whole day there. All the children had to attend Sunday school. When we got older we also went to the morning service or the evening service with the grown-ups, and sometimes I went to both. After the morning service we would all go back to grandparents Withers' home and my grandmother would cook lunch: potatoes, vegetables and always home-baked cakes with jam.

My grandfather was very strict. He believed that Sundays were for talking and conversation and prayer, not for playing football and certainly not for watching television, which was all we kids wanted to do, of course. Not many homes had television sets then. They were a novelty and a luxury and we took every chance we got to look at one. We were even prepared to risk grandfather Withers' hell and damnation to look at it, and we nearly always succeeded. In the afternoon, he would go upstairs and sleep for a couple of hours before the evening service. That is when the television came on and it improved our hearing a hundred percent because we had to keep the sound down as low as possible so as not to disturb him. And one of us always had to sit at the bottom of the stairs and listen for him getting up.

That upbringing obviously left an impression on my eldest sister, Carol. She is married now with two children. She is a kind, gentle person and very religious. She does not have television in the house. And when I took my son, Calum there one Sunday and suggested that he and I and Carol's son who is very keen on football go out and kick a ball around my father took me aside and whispered, 'Not here, not on a Sunday.' I was never as religious as that. But I did have a Bible and I did say the Lord's Prayer before bedtime and I do make Calum do the same. I think it's important.

We never allowed our faith to affect our relations with our neighbours, however. We were Free Presbyterians which, as anyone who knows anything about the sectarian divisions of Northern Ireland will appreciate, is a strict denomination, but we always got on very well with the Catholics who lived nearby. Where I am from and where my family still lives is a mixed estate. Our street was mixed, the social clubs my parents went to were mixed, yet we had no trouble at all.

My mother's best friend was the woman who lived next door. She was Catholic. One of my best friends was one of the 14 Catholic children who lived across the road and we used to go scrumping for apples together in the orchard belonging to the big house at the end of the road (he was a big lad, bigger than me, and I used to use him as a ladder to climb over the wall and then throw the fruit over to him).

The football teams I played in were mixed. The street gangs we formed were mixed. And that's the way I believe it should be. I do what I can to try to bring the two communities together. I went across to Ireland recently for a get together organised to try and bring Catholics and Protestants together and I took Denis Law with me. Denis is a Catholic. I said a few words about how nice it was to be there and how nice it was to have Denis along because it showed that people can mix and that it's not all bad – that there are more nice people than bad people in Northern Ireland. It was a good evening and we enjoyed ourselves.

There was always an undercurrent, though, even when I was a kid, even on the Cregagh. Everyone knew where they belonged. Nothing was obvious or offensive, just the occasional exchange of words. Without really knowing what we were saying we would sometimes hurl religious abuse and insults at each other but most of the time people on the estate got on with their lives and made their friendships without worrying what religion the other person belonged to. Yet in an indirect way it was Belfast's religious barriers that made me into a soccer player.

I was always good at school. I don't think I was ever destined to be an academic and I didn't like subjects like chemistry or geography or history. But I was very good at English and maths. I enjoyed them. I used to look forward to them and in those days the three Rs were the key to a higher education.

Grandfather Withers died the day I took my 11-plus. I was very close to him and they did not tell me what had happened because they didn't want to upset me. I went into a shop to buy some pencils and a rubber and the woman behind the counter asked, 'When's your grandfather getting buried?' I thought she was asking when my grandfather was getting married which was a pretty daft question as he was still living with my grandmother. I did not think any more about it until I got home that evening to a hushed house and I found out what had happened.

I was distraught. I went outside and they found me sitting beneath a lamp post crying my eyes out. But because I had not been told what had happened – and this was the first really upsetting thing that had ever happened to me – the trauma had not affected my exam work and I passed my 11-plus. And passed it well; I was put into the top class at Grosvenor High School.

Grosvenor High is a Protestant grammar school. The problem for me was that it was several miles away from my home – and on the edge of a Catholic area. Because the Cregagh was a mixed estate everyone was forced to get along with everyone else. But that was not true in the sectarian neighbourhoods. There bigotry fed itself and just getting to and from school became a daily nightmare.

My parents never pushed me into anything. My mother had always said that it was up to me what I did with my life. But in their own minds they were very proud when I passed the 11-plus. And I was quite pleased myself. I didn't mind the school. And despite the legend, I didn't mind rugby, which was the game they played at the High School. To be honest, I quite enjoyed it. I played scrum half and I was quite good and who knows, if the school had been closer and these problems had not arisen I might have ended up playing a different kind of football for Ireland.

That wasn't the way it turned out. None of my friends had gone to the grammar school. Most of them had not even bothered to sit the 11-plus. They just went straight into the nearby local secondary modern which meant that I had to make the frightening bus ride across town by myself and face the daily taunts and abuse on my own.

I found myself getting into fights. Not serious fights but worrying enough to an 11-year-old. They knew I was a Protestant by the uniform I was wearing and gangs of Catholic youths would shout at me and chase me down the street and try to snatch my school cap or scarf or my school books. I started timing my run to the bus stop so I got there just as the bus arrived. It was like running a gauntlet and after a few months I stopped bothering. I started playing truant. I would hide my school satchel behind the dustbin at my aunt Margaret's house and spend the day mooching around, kicking a tennis ball around or going into the city centre to look at the shops.

That only made matters worse. Because I wasn't doing my homework my marks were suffering and when I did attend I would be kept back in detention and made to write out lines. That meant that it was late and dark by the time I was let out. There would be no other boys from my school around and I had to make the dash to the bus stop alone. I started spending the money for my bus fare to buy red wine gums in the local sweet shop. I would go and tell my mother that my throat was sore. She would look at my throat and it would be bright red. That trick backfired on me. I tried it once too often and ended up in hospital having my tonsils removed.

It was my aunt Margaret who blew the final whistle on that game. She found my satchel and told my mother and my mother went to the school with me to discuss what was happening. The school gave me the choice – either drop down into one of the lower grades or leave and go to the secondary modern. It seemed ridiculous to me to go down a class. The work wasn't the reason I didn't want to be there – it was the getting there and back that was the problem.

My mother asked me what I wanted to do. I said I would rather go to the secondary modern and be with my friends. I think my parents were very disappointed with me. All parents are ambitious for their children. All parents want to see them do well academically and mine were no exception. But they were not the kind of people to push you into something you didn't want to do. They didn't shout or scream about it. They just repeated that it was up to me to decide what I was going to do with my life.

If I was in the same position with my own son I believe I would do the same thing and let him make the decision. I can see no point in sending a child somewhere where he is going to be very unhappy. I was very unhappy at Manchester United at the end. I was very unhappy at Grosvenor High almost from the start so I left. It was the end of my academic career. It was back to thinking with my feet.

From the time I can first remember, from long before I can remember, all I wanted to do was kick a football. There is a photograph of me aged 14 months with a ball at my feet. Most children can barely walk at that age but there I was, already kicking a football around.

There were other interests in my life. The cinema, the trips to the seaside, the bike rides with my father, school. Soccer didn't dominate my life completely but it certainly made a good attempt. Not that there was much alternative. It was the 1950s and for boys like me, growing up on the Cregagh estate, there was almost nothing else to do. Very few families had television. There were no video games. Holidays consisted of a day trip to Bangor. In the absence of anything else football became the centre of our social life.

We played it at school. We played it after school. We played it at the youth club we went to three evenings a week. We made our friends playing football and my oldest pals, men I still see when I go back to Belfast, are lads I met playing football when I was a boy. We played it every spare minute of the day. I used to run home from school at lunchtime, make myself a couple of pieces of toast and a cup of tea and be back in the playground ten minutes later to join the other boys for a kick around.

As soon as the lessons were finished it was straight back home again for another slice of toast and then out and up to the top of the street where there was a large playing area. You had to be quick. Because there were so many youngsters on the estate the games quickly became 30- or 40- a-side free-for-alls and if you didn't get there early you were lucky if you got a kick. Then, when it got dark and everyone else went home, I would go to the bottom of the street. There were some lock up garages there with a light over them and I would stay there, kicking the ball against the garage door until my mother came looking for me to fetch me indoors and sometimes that would be as late as midnight.

I used to enjoy being sent to the shops because I could take a tennis ball with me and practise things. Come Christmas all I ever wanted was a new football and that is what I got every year; a new ball, a new shirt, shorts, boots and socks. When I was very small, when I was about three or four years old, I even used to take a football to bed with me.

Sometimes my father's father, Grandfather Best who lived a hundred yards away from Glentoran, the local professional side, would take me to watch a match. But I wasn't really bothered whether I went or not. All I really wanted to do was play.

I was a slight lad. My legs were like matchsticks, and I refused to take part in the school gym classes until they gave me a special dispensation to wear a vest because I was embarrassed about how puny I looked. Despite that I was very good at sport. I enjoyed gymnastics and I took part in every event I could at the school sports day – high jump, long jump, 100 yards, 220 yards. And I won most of them.

One year at Nettlefield Primary I would probably have won them all (except the high jump where my lack of height was against me) had it not been for my embarrassment over my physique. I'd already won the long jump and went straight into the 100 yards afterwards. The other boys were stripped down. I was wearing an ordinary white school shirt and I would not take it off. We crouched down and the starter said, 'On your marks, get set – go.' Everyone did –

Aged 14 months with a football at my feet, outside Granny Withers' House in Donald Street, Belfast.

me. The wind caught my shirt and turned it into a sail. I tried to run but I couldn't; the wind was blowing me back. I finished last.

But while I liked these other sports they never diverted my enthusiasm from football. I lived for it.

There's an explanation for this boyhood obsession. When you're good at something, especially something everybody else around wants to be good at, you have the incentive to devote a lot of time to it. And I was the best footballer in the neighbourhood. By a long way and from a very early age. Even the big kids couldn't get the ball off me. I used to run rings around them.

Aged 21 with a football at my feet in front of 54,000 people at Old Trafford, Manchester. (© S. K. Fraser, Camera Press)

After Grosvenor High I went to Lisnasharragh Intermediate, a secondary modern production-line grinding out its endless quota of ill-educated manual workers. This was the school where my friends were and no one was much concerned with academic achievement. Everyone was just waiting to be old enough to leave. The girls were interested in boys and make-up and getting a job in the local hairdressers or Woolies. The boys talked about the girls, and how their dads were going to fix them up with a job at the yards – and about football.

19

I wasn't having much luck with the girls because I was so small. And I wasn't having much luck with my football for the same reason. I played for the school team. I played for the Cregagh Boys Club and sometimes I was playing two or even three games on a Saturday. Belfast has always been a source of raw soccer talent and there were always scouts from the Irish and the big English clubs at the games and at the back of my mind I was always hoping that someone standing on the touchline would spot me and sign me up then and there.

But no one took much interest in me, even if I went out and scored a couple of goals, which I usually did. All they said was: 'Oh, he's too small, he'll never make it.'

By the time Bob Bishop came to look at me I had given up dreaming of ever becoming a professional football player. Bishop ran a club called Boyland, which was the top youth club for soccer in Northern Ireland. He was also a scout for Manchester United from way back. He would later send Sammy McIlroy and Norman Whiteside over to Old Trafford, so he wasn't a bad judge of footballers; and he liked what he saw in me.

Without telling me what he was doing, when I was 15 he arranged a special match between Cregagh Boys Club and his Boyland side, which was full of 18-year-olds, to see if I could stand up to the rigours. We beat them 4-2, and I scored twice. A few days later my father called me into the house and said there was a man who wanted to talk to me. It was Bishop. It was the week after I'd passed the examination to become a printer's apprentice. Bishop said: 'Do you want to play for Manchester United?'

I went back up the field to where the other lads were kicking a ball around and said, 'I've just signed for Manchester United.' They said, 'Oh sure, pull the other one,' or words to that effect. But it was true. Sir Matt Busby always said, 'If they're good enough they are big enough', and Bishop had seen everything he wanted to see.

He had sent a telegram that night after the match. It simply said, 'I have found a genius.'

Chapter Two

United

I T WAS TWO very small, very frightened little boys who took the ferry from Belfast and set sail for Liverpool that day in 1961. I was 15 and travelling with another boy of my age named Eric McMordie. We were going to spend a two-week trial period with the greatest club in Britain and we were petrified. Neither of us had ever been more than 15 miles outside Belfast before. I had never worn long trousers before: my mother had gone out and bought me my first pair especially for the journey. We didn't even have a clear idea of where we were going. Our instructions had been: get to Liverpool, get the train to Manchester, get a cab and tell them, 'Old Trafford', and we'll meet you when you get there.

We did as we were told. We got to Manchester. We got into a taxi, the first taxi we had ever been in, and said, 'Old Trafford, please.' The driver asked, 'Which Old Trafford?' Neither of us was aware that there was also a cricket ground called Old Trafford. We were very confused and very shy, and this hardly did wonders for our confidence. It took another battering when we got to the ground. To try and make us feel at home the coaches introduced us to the juniors. But they were all a year or two older than us. They had had at least a year of training and building up and were a lot bigger than us. And if they were frightening, the professionals were terrifying.

We were taken to say hello to the Irish players at the club. We were introduced to Harry Gregg, the great United goalkeeper who had survived the Munich air crash. He towered over us. He stood six foot something and was built like a concrete pillar. He looked like an Amazon compared to us. The club put us up in digs with a lady called Mrs Fullaway. That night Eric and I sat up talking. He said, 'I don't want to stay.' I said I was scared. We hummed and hah-ed about it. We were a bit worried about missing our opportunity – it isn't every day that someone comes along and says, 'Do you want to play for Manchester United? Now's your chance.'

But in the end we decided that this was not for us, and first thing next morning we went and told the chief scout, a fellow called Joe Armstrong, that we wanted to go home.

Homesickness was a part of our thinking; we had never been away from home before except to stay with relatives and Manchester was a big, intimidating place. I was bad enough; Eric was worse. I also had another worry. I was unsure of myself then. I really didn't think that I was good enough to make it. Throughout my schooldays I had been told that I was too small, too weak, too skinny ever to make it in professional football. All the big Irish clubs had passed me over, and if I wasn't good enough for them, how could I possibly be good enough for Manchester United?

Armstrong was not very impressed when we told him that we were going home. He told us not to be stupid. He told us that the biggest club in the world was giving us a chance and that we would be crazy, mad, to throw that away because, what, 'You're homesick?' He made us feel pathetic and, looking back, I suppose we were. But we insisted and that day we were back on the ferry and on our way home to Belfast.

I hadn't told my mother or father what I was doing, and they weren't very pleased to see me when I walked back through the door I had walked out of only a few hours earlier and 12 days before the trial period was due to end. They asked me what I was doing home. I said: 'We didn't like it there, we wanted to come home.' My father thought that I had got myself into trouble and shouted at me, 'What the hell have you done?' He thought I had been kicked out so he telephoned Old Trafford and spoke to Sir Matt and asked him what the problem was. Sir Matt told him what I had told him, that we were homesick. My father took me aside and had a long chat with me. He asked me if I was sure I was doing the right thing. I said I wasn't. He asked me if I wanted to go back and try again. Rather sheepishly I said I would. He telephoned United for me and they agreed to give me another chance; and two weeks later I was back on the boat again, alone this time, and on my way to Old Trafford for a second attempt. Which was all very silly and childish when you remember that I had only just walked out on them.

No one was writing about a George Best walk-out then, of course. No one was writing about George Best at all. I was just another nervous hopeful, one of the thousands of youngsters who get a trial with the big clubs every year. Most of them never get past that first stage and just in case I turned out to be one of the ones who didn't my father made arrangements to keep my printing apprenticeship open.

It is a tough, ruthless system and it is not perfect. David Platt of Aston Villa was thrown out of United because they did not think he was good enough. Now he is in the England squad. Eric McMordie did not get another chance with United though he did eventually sign for Middlesborough and go on to win himself a place in the Northern Ireland international squad with me. I was luckier. I may not have been big but no one had ever denied my talent. The coaches liked what they saw and despite my size I was kept on. Illegally, as it turned out.

In those days if you came from Scotland or Ireland you couldn't sign an apprentice form with an English club. The Scottish and Irish football authorities had complained about the way the big English teams had been poaching their best young talent and by the time I got there it had been agreed that the only way a lad from Ireland could be attached to a club like United was as an amateur.

That meant that I had to get a job and I went to work as a clerk at the Manchester Ship Canal Company. I was only able to train on Tuesdays and Thursdays. I complained. I said I had come to Manchester to play football, not to run around making tea. I said that I wanted to train every day with the other apprentices. They said that was not allowed. When I persisted the club said that it would look into it.

What it did was persuade a man who ran an electrical suppliers to 'employ' me, along with a Scots lad named John Fitzpatrick who would also go on to play for the first team. Under that under-the-counter arrangement we clocked in at nine o'clock in the morning and then walked out the back and on to the training ground. We got back to the storeroom at five o'clock in time to clock off. I don't know if United paid the man for his help. If it did, it was certainly more than it was paying me.

Bob Bishop received £100 for spotting me. My parents were not paid any money for my signature, the way so many parents are today. My first wage was £4.1s.9d. I sent

£3 home to my mother to help towards the family. That left me with £1.1s.9d. It was not very much, even then, though to a 15-year-old from a Belfast council estate it seemed a lot. Not that the money mattered. I was just delighted to be there. I loved it. It was all I had ever dreamed of and as I settled in my confidence began to build.

We used to train at a training ground called the Cliff and I trained harder than anyone because I enjoyed it and because I wanted to do well. I had been a little worried at first. On my first few times out I looked around at the other players. One would be playing in the reserves, another in the first team, another in the A team, someone else in the B. They all looked bigger and so much better than me and I figured to myself, 'It's going to take you 20 years to make it into the first team.' Then we went out on those long-distance runs the coaches made us do and all those players I had been so worried about cheated. As soon as we came out of the ground and turned right half the squad would turn left and go and hide behind the bushes and have a cigarette.

None of those players ever really made it and when I saw them doing that I knew I was in with a real chance. And I worked for it. People say that I never trained. That annoys me. I did. I came back every afternoon and practised on my own for hours. I enjoyed it. I enjoyed everything about my life then. I made friends. I settled into Manchester. I even found the time to have my first affair. It was with a girl called Maria. She was the girlfriend of Steve, the son of Mrs Fullaway, my landlady. He had taken her out a few times and one night, when the three of us were walking to the fish and chip shop, I slipped her a note asking her to meet me the next day.

Steve found the note, which was a bit unfortunate and he was not very pleased, but he got over that and a couple of weeks later I took her out. Her aunt owned a cake shop in Manchester and we went to bed for the first time in the flat above the store. Then we rushed downstairs again and helped ourselves to cakes. The bridgehead was established and for the next few months I used to go round and babysit with her for her aunt and uncle and enjoy sessions between the cakes and cakes between the sessions.

There were casual encounters with other girls – hurried

affairs in the back seat of someone's car, fumbles in doorways, all the usual teenage things with all the usual teenage problem of nowhere to go. It was a case of taking whatever opportunity you found. They were usually living at home. I was living in digs and I was supposed to be back by eleven o'clock.

I didn't always make it and when I didn't I borrowed a ladder out of the next door neighbour's garden and climbed in through the bedroom window. That was all right for me. It wasn't all right for Steve Fullaway. We were sharing a bedroom and I kept crashing down on top of him. After a while Mrs Fullaway gave up and gave me my own key to the front door. She was not supposed to: the club had strict rules about the time its apprentices had to be at home and in bed. But she had a soft spot for me. She told me to come and go as I pleased and promised not to tell Sir Matt about it (not that she had to – he had a pretty shrewd idea of what I and all the other apprentices were up to).

I had just fallen in love then for the first time with a girl I had seen at the bowling alley. I was shy and it took me days before I plucked up the courage to go across to speak to her. Night after night I sat there, sipping a Coca Cola, too afraid to say anything, hoping that she might say something to me, looking at my watch to make sure I wasn't going to get home too late. Eventually she smiled at me and we started talking. She said that she was distantly related to an actress called June Ritchie who was doing quite well at the time. We started going out on dates together – to the pictures, for fish and chips, back to the bowling alley.

I felt rather pleased with myself. At that time my friends were Steve (he had got over the Maria incident by then) and Dave Sadler, who had just signed for United and Jim Ryan, who is now the manager of Luton, and John Fitzpatrick. They had fancied her too but I was the lucky one, I was the one who had her. Or so I thought: when I turned up at her digs to take her out one night the woman who answered the door told me that she'd run away to marry a sailor.

I bumped into her some ten years later and she was really struggling. She said that she had gone through rough times with the sailor and she looked as if she had; and I felt sorry for her. At the time she left me, though, I was too busy feeling sorry for myself to worry about anything else. I was heart-broken. It was my first real love affair and I sulked around for days afterwards, playing James Dean and not speaking to anybody. At that age, though, you get over things like that very quickly. At that age girls don't matter very much. You think they do but you are really more interested in hanging around with your mates, playing snooker, going bowling, being one of the lads.

And then, of course, there was football. I talked it. I dreamed it. I watched it. I played it. Without really being aware of it happening I was getting better and better at it, and I made it into the youth team which was an achievement in those days. I didn't think any further than the next game.

My father was more practical. I was 16 years old and I'd been at Old Trafford for almost two years. He was worried about me. He didn't know if I was going to make it and he probably thought I wouldn't and there are very few prospects for a football reject with only a rudimentary education.

In 1963 United played Leicester City in the F.A. Cup Final. United, as was the custom then, took everybody along to Wembley to see the match. My father came over from Belfast and he was very concerned. He tried to persuade me to come home and get myself a proper job. That line of argument didn't get him very far so he insisted on going to see Sir Matt and asking him what was going to happen. Sir Matt said: 'We're going to sign him as a professional on his birthday.'

I turned 17 a couple of weeks after United won the F.A. Cup. That was in May. Four months later, on 14 September, 1963, I made my First Division debut against West Bromwich Albion. Then I dropped out again. But I had left an impression. The *Manchester Evening News* reported that I 'played pluckily and finished the game in style'. The report also mentioned what it called my 'natural talent'.

Sir Matt was not in any rush to bring me in, however. He had a good team, one that had just won the Cup and I didn't play again until three days after Boxing Day. It was against Burnley which was a First Division side then and a useful one at that – it had won the First Division championship three seasons before.

Because Manchester and Burnley are so close, the fixture

list was arranged so that when we were in the same division we met twice, home and away, in the space of a few days over the Christmas period. I didn't play in the first match at Burnley and I was given permission to go back to Belfast to spend Christmas with my family.

Burnley slaughtered United 5-1 in the first game and the following day I received a telegram from the club informing me that I was required back in Manchester. My father said: 'Next game you're going to play in the first team.'

I said, no, I wasn't, they've probably had a couple of injuries and they just want me for cover.

'No,' he said, 'you're going to play.'

I telephoned the club and said that of course I was happy to come back to Manchester but that I wanted to get back to Belfast straight after the game. I was not being difficult or tricky. I was 17 years old and I desperately wanted to play. But I also wanted to spend Christmas with my family. The club agreed. They said, all right, but get here.

I did. I played. United beat Burnley 5-1. I scored the first goal, my first goal in the Football League. I felt marvellous. I remember walking out of the tunnel and hearing the roar of 54,000 people. The tunnel at Old Trafford is on a slope and as you walk down you can see the crowd opening out in front of you. When the first spectators see you they start to cheer and the noise spreads around the whole stadium in an instant, getting louder and louder. It is like turning on a radio and turning the volume up. One moment there is silence. The next you are swamped in an amphitheatre of noise. I can still recall the way the hairs on the back of my neck stood up. I was numbed. At the same time I felt exhilarated. There was no fear, however, not for a moment. And there never would be. I was born to this.

Many players suffer the most dreadful attacks of nerves before a match. It is the athletic equivalent of stage fright and they develop their eccentric little routines to overcome them. Nobby Stiles would come in, take his teeth out, put his contacts in, check his kit and then check it again. In all it would take him an hour getting ready. Bobby Charlton had a couple of shots of whisky before he went out. Alan Gowling was sick, violently sick. He would throw up in the toilet before every game. Brian Kidd was the same.

I would arrive, pick up a programme and take it into the toilet and read it. I would come out and walk out of the dressing room and go and talk to my friends outside.

That is the way it always was. That is what I did before the Burnley game. Twenty minutes before the kick-off a search party was mounted to look for me. It found me outside in the car park drinking a cup of tea. That was just the way I was. It panicked Sir Matt. He was always asking, 'Where's George?'

The style of my pre-match preparation was established at that match and it stayed like that for the rest of my playing career. In those early days, despite Sir Matt's concern, there was nothing to worry about. I was not getting myself waylaid on the way to the ground. I always turned up. I wanted to turn up. I wanted to play football and playing football never caused me any anxiety. The problems would come later, off the field, and when they did Sir Matt had every reason to worry. But not then, not when it was fun and the most exciting thing I could possibly have been doing.

It was also easy, just as easy as it had been on the streets of the Cregagh estate. I discovered that I could go past the big men, the hard, seasoned professionals with big reputations, with the same ease I had gone round the bigger boys I played against as a child; and I revelled in it. The night before a match I would lie in bed and plot what I was going to do on the field the next day. I used to imagine myself pushing the ball between the legs of the defender who I knew would be marking me; and the next day I would go out and do it.

I once saw Alan Ball trap the ball with his backside and I thought, 'If he can do that, so can I,' so I went out and did it. On another occasion I ran through on my own, stopped the ball on the line, bent down and headed it in for a goal. I did it to make people laugh, because I thought it was funny.

It didn't always amuse the players I was playing with. When I first got into the team I was playing with people of the calibre of Bobby Charlton and Nobby Stiles, Denis Law, Paddy Crerand, all of them internationals. They would be screaming for the ball but I always wanted it for myself. You could call it selfishness but it was just a hangover from my days on the Cregagh where, if you got the ball, the idea was to hang on to it until someone managed to take it off

you. In my case they rarely did. I was a greedy little urchin.
I would not pass.

I learned from experience, of course. I learned to release
the ball to a player in a better position and then run through,
making space for the return. But at heart I always remained
a kid. When I got the ball I wanted to keep it for as long as I
could. I never subscribed to Sir Alf Ramsey's doctrine of hard
running off the ball. I am a footballer – and that means having
a football at my feet.

That was how Sir Matt believed the game should be played
and I must have been doing something right because, after
that Burnley game, I was in the side for the rest of the season.
And United let me go back to Belfast straight after the match.
They flew me home. I travelled home by aeroplane – I had
always travelled by boat before – so I knew I was in the big
time. I couldn't wait to read the newspapers the next day. I
can still remember the thrill I felt to see my name in print.
There would come a time when I would dread picking up a
paper but that was away in the future. It was all fresh then,
and so was I.

I was still technically a junior, however, and even though
I was now a member of the first team squad I still continued
to play in the youth team. A lot of professionals would have
found that degrading. I didn't. I would have played every day
if there had been a match to play in and I was almost as
happy turning out with the other youngsters as I was running
down the tunnel of Old Trafford with the likes of Law and
Charlton.

There was not that much difference in atmosphere, anyway. We won the F.A. Youth Cup in 1964 and when we
played Swindon over two legs in the final the crowds were up
around the 30,000 mark which are the sort of gates most First
Division sides would be very happy with today. It was good,
rousing stuff and I had the added bonus of looking forward
to the write-ups that were starting to come with every game
I played in.

The Belfast papers picked me up first with the obvious
local-boy-makes-good stories. Then the national newspapers
started writing about George Best, the new Busby Babe.
I was flattered. I started a scrap book of my press cut-
tings. I liked it when people asked me for autographs.

What I did not have was the faintest inkling where all this would lead.

Without realising it I would become a monster to myself. I was a kid from Belfast who had never been more than a few miles outside of the city before I took the boat across to Liverpool and the train up to Manchester. Then, 24 months after leaving school, I was playing in front of 54,000 at Old Trafford, doing something I wanted to do and getting very well paid for it.

That first season in the first team I got £17 a week. The second year, at a time when someone like Denis Law was on around £200 basic, it went up to £125. But there were also bonuses. There was a crowd bonus, a win bonus, a bonus for being in the top six. When you added it all together it came to close to a £1,000 a week which was a fortune in those days and is still an impressive wage today. I felt like a millionaire; and when the advertising endorsements started flooding in I was.

I bought a car, an Austin. Then I bought a Lotus and gave the Austin to my father. After that it was E-types, a succession of them, one after the other and, looking at the prices they fetch today, I wish I still had them. I also became interested in clothes. In 1967 I opened a boutique called Edwardia with my friend Mike Summerbee who played for Manchester City, selling crushed velvet jackets and paisley shirts and all the other stuff that was fashionable at the time.

That was the way it was in the '60s. Everyone was 'doing their own thing' and I was in there, right at the beginning of it all. It was a time of experimentation and change in fashion and hairstyles and music and they even wrote a pop song about me. The pill was coming in, which led to the sexual revolution of which I was one of the major beneficiaries – or victims, depending on which way you look at it.

The springboard for all this was football and it was a glorious time to play the game. The sport was full of great characters like Stan Bowles, Rodney Marsh, Charlie George, Alan Ball, Eddie Gray, Peter Osgood and, of course, Law and Charlton, people you were happy to spend money to see. And, at United at least, you were not bound in to any rigid tactical system. We played two full backs, three half backs and five forwards. It was not complicated and it was not meant to be.

George Best the businessman – at the opening of one of my clothes boutiques. It would have helped if I'd known what I was doing. (© Nancy Holmes, Camera Press)

Football at its best is a simple game. You need people at the back who can tackle, midfielders who can pass and forwards who can control, shoot straight and score goals. As soon as you start talking numbers instead of positions, like they do today, you know there's something not right. We never talked about how we were going to play. We just went out onto the pitch and got on with it.

Sir Matt didn't spend much time giving team talks. He was not like Billy Bingham or Danny Blanchflower who managed the Northern Ireland sides I played for. Their team talks seemed to go on for hours. All Sir Matt would say was 'Watch their winger', or 'The full backs are vulnerable.' He might take me aside and say, 'Look out for so and so, he's going to kick you.' He got his points over as quickly as he could and then told us to go out and enjoy ourselves and do what came naturally.

It worked. At our best we were audacious and flamboyant, dangerous and unpredictable. We were, quite simply, the most exciting team this country has ever produced and people flocked to see us. It was a team of great players and Busby knew it. We all knew where we were going and who was going to be there alongside us. If someone had blown a whistle and stopped the game, blindfolded me and asked me to indicate where every player on my team was I could have told him.

All great athletes can do that because they're always thinking ahead. I'm sure that Steve Davis doesn't think about the snooker ball he's about to play; he's thinking five, ten shots ahead. It's the same in soccer. Law and Charlton and Crerand were always thinking about the next move, and the one after that, weighing up the possibilities and the opportunities. It didn't always work, of course, and there was a lot of shouting on the field if you made a mistake or gave a bad pass. But it was all very relaxed. We were a great team and we knew it. And, on the field at least, we all got on very well – if you're playing with the best you appreciate what they're doing and you applaud them for it.

That didn't mean that we were not competitive. We were. There were sometimes punch-ups during training. Denis Law hit Bill Foulkes once, Foulkes did a fair bit of hitting himself and you certainly didn't want to annoy big

Harry Gregg. Harry was not what you would call a mild-tempered man.

No one held back during the practice sessions. We used to play six and seven-a-side games between ourselves down at the Stretford End of Old Trafford where the pylons for the floodlights are. There was broken glass and stones on the ground and concrete pillars to stop people driving onto the pitch. We used the pillars as goal posts and got stuck in, smashing each other onto the ground and into the pillars, all the time kicking the hell out of each other. There were no favours asked and certainly none given. And this was a team made of players who, by today's inflated prices, were worth three, four and, perhaps in my case, as much as five or six million pounds. But no matter what happened or who got hurt, there were no complaints afterwards. If someone hit someone nobody heard about it. We kept our troubles to ourselves. We were men. Afterwards you shook hands.

The boss let us get on with it. Sir Matt was always very relaxed about things. The only thing he was interested in was how well you performed on the park. If you'd played well he always let you know. He loved to pull on a track suit and spend a few minutes kicking a ball around with his players during the training sessions. In the course of the morning he would walk past you and say, 'Well done on Saturday.' He did that to me on the Monday after that game against Burnley. He tapped me on the elbow and said, 'Well done, son.' I felt as if Jesus Christ had spoken to me

The only time he showed his anger was if we had played particularly badly. If we'd tried our best and still lost he would simply say, 'Forget about it.' If the fault was ours, however, if we had lost concentration or got ourselves involved in needless scuffles or not pulled our weight, he would sit us down in the dressing room and say a few crisp, sharp words to the whole team. He didn't raise his voice but you were left in no doubt as to what he thought. He would also make his point to individual players. He didn't embarrass anyone by telling them off in front of the others. He would call whoever had not played well into his office on Monday morning.

The first time he called me in I could not figure out what he wanted to see me about. He said, 'Sit down.' Then he asked me: 'How do you think you played on Saturday?' That

33

put the ball firmly in my court, which was Busby's way of handling these situations. I was honest. I said that I hadn't played well.

He asked me if I had any idea why. He said: 'I hope it has nothing to do with this brown cow.'

'You mean the Brown Bull, boss?' which was the pub we all drank in, as if he didn't know.

'Yes, that one.'

I said that it was not; that it had just been one of those off days which every athlete gets once in a while. He said: 'Good, that's fine then.' It was excellent psychology – he knew that the following Saturday I would be out there doing my damnedest for the team.

There wasn't really very much cause for complaint in those days, though. In 1965 we won the League title for the first time in eight years. In 1967 we won it again. In the 1965-66 season we had stormed through the European Cup, demolishing the supposedly unbeatable Benfica team 5-1 in Lisbon, before going out to Partizan Belgrade in the semi-finals. The gates at Old Trafford were the best in the league and we never really had away games – at times our supporters outnumbered the home supporters at away matches. We were the side that everyone wanted to see. And along the way I had established myself without question or exaggeration as one of the most exciting footballers in the world.

To my great regret, though, United never made it to an F.A. Cup final while I was there. We came close. The next game after Burnley was against Southampton in the cup. I was 17. There was another lad there called Willie Anderson who was still only 16. Sir Matt decided to play us both. The press said he should not, that it was folly to pitch two kids into such an important match. The boss's answer was that we had proved ourselves and he was proved right: we won 3-2, which is a lesson a lot of managers today might do well to remember. In the semi-finals we were drawn against West Ham United.

The other semi-final was between Swansea and Preston North End, who had a youngster called Howard Kendall in their side. Howard was born on the same day as me. We lost. Preston won and Howard, who went on to manage Everton, Athletico Bilbao and Manchester City, had the distinction

At Manchester United's Cliff training ground, reading my fan mail which arrived by the sackful every day. (© Camera Press)

of being the youngest player to appear at Wembley in an F.A. final.

That disappointment aside, it had been one long glorious run. Except for one missing thing: the European Cup. All great clubs have ambition. At United it was more than that. It was a mission, a crusade underwritten by the blood of the players who died in the Munich air crash in 1958 on their way back from their quarter-final win over Red Star Belgrade.

We didn't sit around talking about it. Yet there was an aura about Old Trafford. It was as if the ghosts of the Busby Babes were still around the place and we all knew what was expected of us. It was even more pressing for players like Charlton and Foulkes who had been aboard the airliner when it crashed. They had seen their colleagues die in the pursuit of the Cup, the greatest club prize in football. They wanted to win it desperately – for their own satisfaction, obviously, but also for the men who had died.

For Sir Matt Busby it was nothing less than his life's ambition. He had been badly hurt in the crash and at one time it looked as if he wouldn't be able to continue as manager. But he did, and it was the search for the Holy Grail of victory in Europe that kept him going. And in 1966 we thought we had it within our grasp. Charlton, Law and Crerand were in their prime and the team was at its peak. We were unstoppable.

Playing in Europe was always special. It was the icing on the cake of your work. The atmosphere was different: tenser and more exciting. I also happen to like travelling, which added to my enjoyment. It was different for Charlton and Foulkes. They had been aboard the plane that had crashed in Munich and it took courage to get into an aircraft again after that. They never said anything when we flew off somewhere. They didn't have to. You could see what they were thinking: it was written large on their faces, on Bill's especially. But they were not going to give up or back out. They had a job to complete and they knew, we all knew, that this was the side that was going to do it.

A lot of teams are apprehensive when they go abroad. They go away hoping for a bit of luck to earn them a draw. That was not how we felt. We travelled with confidence. We believed that every time we stepped out onto a pitch we had a chance of winning. And when we crushed Benfica in 1966 in front of

75,000 of their own fans we were convinced that the trophy was ours. That was a wonderful game. Benfica had played 18 home matches in European competition in the previous six years – and had won every one of them. They were regarded as the most formidable team in Europe. And in Eusebio they had one of the world's greatest players.

We had beaten them 3-2 in the first leg at Old Trafford and Sir Matt, being cautious for once, told us to take it easy, not to get carried away in attack and expose our defence. So what did I do? I went out and scored two goals in the first 12 minutes and we went on to win 5-1. The man from *The Times*, not a newspaper given to overstatement, called it one of the greatest performances of all time by a British club. Sir Matt's remark, referring to me, was: 'I wish he wouldn't listen to me more often.'

I had a feeling of total warmth afterwards. That is the only way I can describe how I felt when I walked off the field at the end of the game, knowing that I had done something that no one else could have done or is ever likely to do again. I was labelled El Beatle and I was suddenly the best-known sportsman in Britain. I was also on my way to becoming the richest. Unfortunately, United were not on their way to winning the European Cup, not that year at any rate. I was having cartilage problems in my right knee. In the middle of a game it would lock up and I would have to come off. It was in urgent need of an operation but the boss asked me if, rather than having it seen to straightaway, I minded carrying on playing for as long as we remained in the European Cup. I agreed, but it was a painful struggle. After every match I had to put ice packs on my knee to bring the swelling down. Afterwards I would be given some heat treatment and it would be all right for a few days. All we were doing, however, was delaying the inevitable, and in the first leg of the semi-final in, of all places, Belgrade, against Partizan it went completely. We lost the match 2-0. I was not able to play in the return at Old Trafford. Belgrade closed the game down. United were unable to open it up and only managed to win 1-0. It wasn't enough and we were out.

Getting knocked out of any Cup competition is bad enough. Getting knocked out of the European Cup feels like the end of the world. You just want to crawl into a corner and die.

Some of the players tried to put a brave face on it by saying things like, 'Well, there'll always be a next time.' For some there would be. Others were not so certain.

Sir Matt was devastated. He said later: 'I was at the lowest ebb since the Munich air crash and it was in my mind to turn my back on football altogether. It seemed the fates had conspired against the club and myself and I remember telling Paddy Crerand: 'We'll never win the European Cup now.'

Paddy didn't agree with him. Nor did I. I always had a feeling that we would win it one day. I didn't have an obsession about it, like the boss did; I just felt instinctively that because of what happened at Munich, if any English club was going to win the Cup it was going to be us.

It was going to be a long, hard uphill struggle, however. We were going to have to win the League again in order to qualify for the competition. And, on a more personal front, I had my knee injury to deal with. These days a cartilage operation is relatively simple, with little chance of complications. In those days they had to slit your knee open, extract the cartilage and sew you up again. You never knew if it was going to be successful and even if it was you needed five or six weeks off to recuperate.

My operation was not a success. The knee didn't feel right. It did not respond to physiotherapy. I didn't feel as if it was ever going to get better and like all athletes with a nagging physical problem, I started suffering the dark fear that my career might be over. I asked Sir Matt for permission to go to Belfast to see Bobby McGregor, a trainer with the Northern Ireland team who was regarded as something of a magician at treating such ailments.

Permission was refused but I went to see Bobby anyway. He gave me a piece of wood to bite on, dug his fingers deep into the back of my knee and wrenched the ligaments back into place. It worked – a week later I was back playing again. The pain is still there, though. It gets worse every year and when I was playing on the dry, hard pitches in the United States I would often end a game in tears. The pain in my ankle caused by the wear and tear that is the inevitable consequence of playing professional football was not getting any less, either. They are the battle wounds I sustained in Manchester United's cause. They were not injuries enough

*The "Boss" and I. Sir Matt Busby and I with the "Holy Grail",
the European Cup. I am holding the British Player of the Year
Award.*

to stop me playing, however. We won the League again that
season and I played in every game. And in 1968 we finally
climbed up the last hill and won the European Cup.

It was the fulfilment of a dream and I am sure that Sir
Matt actually used to go to bed at night and dream about
it. Brian Kidd cried. So too did Bobby Charlton. Outwardly
Bill Foulkes was cool and calm as if it had been just another
game, but deep down he was as excited as everyone else. Sir
Matt wandered around with this beatific look on his face for
days afterwards.

I went out and got drunk; to be quite honest I don't remember very much about the victory night. I was celebrating and
I had every reason to. The skinny, shy little boy who came
off the ferry from Belfast seven years before had done his job.
And more: if you look at the results leading up to the game at
Wembley, at the goals that were scored and who scored them,
at the final itself, you will see the contribution I made.

It adds up to one thing: if I hadn't been playing for
them I don't think Manchester United would have won
the European Cup.

Chapter Three

A Rare Talent

I WAS BORN with a talent other people would have died for. I could do things that no other footballer had ever been able to do and I could do them easily. I knew I was different. I felt different. And if in the end I became a monster to myself, I gave millions of people hours of pleasure for years.

When I was out on the pitch I would think about the people who had paid hard-earned money to see me play. I used to think of the fathers there with their sons and the disappointment they would be feeling if the game came towards its end and the team they supported was losing.

I remember one game. It was against West Bromwich Albion at Old Trafford and we were losing 1-0 with only a few minutes to go. The fathers were frustrated. The kids were upset. You could see it on their faces when you got close to the touchline and I had had plenty of time to study them because I had hardly had a kick that game. Then in the last five minutes I scored two quite spectacular goals and we won the match 2-1.

I wasn't happy, however. I sat in the bar afterwards feeling displeased with myself because I had not played well. Then I thought, why am I upset? With ten minutes to go 50,000 people were on the point of going home miserable and disappointed. And within five minutes I'd completely turned the game around. I'd done it with flair and skill, and that's what the people had paid to see.

Skills like mine didn't materialise out of thin air, however. Sir Matt Busby said that I was the most naturally gifted footballer he had ever seen, and I'm not going to argue with the Boss. But it requires hard work and dedication and constant practice to turn natural talent into match-winning ability. It would be easy to look back and say that all I had to do was walk out onto the pitch and let nature take over; but it was never quite as easy as that. When I was starting out I put in hours of extra work in order to do what I wanted to do.

It started when I was a young boy. When I was sent to the shops I'd always take a tennis ball with me and practise things with it. I'd hit it against garage doors. When I had learned how to control the rebound I started hitting it against the curb, so that it would bounce back quicker. And when I had mastered that I started kicking it against doorknobs. That was difficult because a ball comes back off a doorknob in all sorts of directions. The trick is to strike it so that it hits the centre of the doorknob and comes back straight to you.

My apprenticeship continued at Old Trafford. We only trained in the morning but instead of going off after lunch with the other lads to the snooker halls or the bowling alleys, I would go back to do extra work on my own. I would go out with ten or 12 balls and practise kicking them into the goal. Which was fine except that after a few minutes I had to go and fish them all out of the net again. So I started practising kicking them against the crossbar. From the penalty spot, then from 20 yards, then from 30, then from 40. After I had mastered that I started working on my weaker left foot.

That's one of the things that so upsets me about the way the game is played today. All too often you see a player get into a scoring position and then failing to hit the target – from 15, 12, even eight yards. There is absolutely no excuse for that. They are professionals who earn their livelihood kicking a football, and the paying public has an absolute right to expect them to be able to get a shot on target from those distances. I can still do it. I can still hit the crossbar from 20 yards and I get very annoyed with myself if I fail to do it nine times out of ten. It's simply a matter of practice.

It's the same with controlling a ball. When I was teaching myself I would set myself little tasks like kicking the ball from 40 yards with just the right weight on it so that it stopped within six inches of the corner flag. And I kept working on my left foot until it actually became stronger than my right one. It was a personal test. For instance, I played a game in Fort Lauderdale in Florida and I told some friends of mine who were watching that I wouldn't touch the ball with my right foot for the whole 90 minutes. And I didn't. I doubt that any player in Britain today could do that. I know that they wouldn't be allowed to. A terrible fear has crept into our game.

To put it bluntly, our coaching is wrong, our training is wrong, the way we play the game is wrong. Everybody trains the same. There is no individuality. Skill has been replaced by running and hard work; and they are no substitutes at all. This terrible failing has worked its way down to the boys' level. The kids are having the individuality coached out of them. It's replaced by fear; the fear of losing, of making a fool of yourself.

The pressures of the modern game are partly responsible for this depressing trend. The money available today is phenomenal. When I was playing the money was good but nothing like it is now, even allowing for inflation. We never talked in millions and millions; now you can't buy a defender for under a couple of million pounds. Players insist that that doesn't matter, that they don't allow their price tags to worry them. But they must, especially in places like Italy and Spain where the fans are screaming blood. And if the club has just paid four or five million pounds for you and you are not performing well it must start preying on your mind.

Yet despite that the Continentals still manage to produce the quality of football every fan has the right to expect. Look at the Dutchman, Ruud Gullit, who plays for A.C. Milan. He's a great player by any standards. He has all the skills. He's not afraid to do things with the ball. And he looks as if he's enjoying every second of it.

By my reckoning that's what makes him an even better player than Maradona. Both have the key quality you will find in all the best players: balance. You just can't knock them off the ball. It was the same with Pele, Beckenbauer and Cruyff. They all had excellent balance and if you are going in for a tackle or challenging for a 50/50 ball, the player with the better balance stands a better chance. He's going to be on his feet, not off them. And when he does fall, he falls well.

Here, I believe, lies the problem with Bryan Robson, and explains why he has accumulated such a catalogue of injuries. Commentators call him a great player and in the all-round sense he is. But he does not have the balance that allows players like Maradona to ride the physical side of the game the way that Maradona does. Nor does he have

Maradona's charisma. Robson is a nice lad and an excellent professional. But he's not the kind of player that people are going to make a special effort to go and watch. Football fans pay to watch individuals. They enjoy a bit of character, a bit of nastiness even, and quite apart from his vunerability to injury, Bryan is simply too nice to be put into the highest class. Maradona most certainly is in that class, though I do sometimes think that he plays because it is his job and not because he's in love with the game the way Pele was.

But if that is a reservation it is a small one compared to the players currently being offered to the British footballing public. The Italians are given the skills of Maradona, Gullit and van Basten. The British have the long ball. With it Dave Bassett took Wimbledon from the Fourth Division to the First. But does his team's success really justify the means? The long ball is crude and uncultured. Worst of all it's boring; and Dave Bassett's, Howard Wilkinson's and (in his Watford days) Graham Taylor's way of playing is a disgrace. It takes all the poetry out of the game. It sacrifices skill for brute force – for Fourth Division sides can kick as far as First Division sides. It levels everything out which is why teams from the lower divisions are beating the top sides with increasing regularity. Which is fine if you happen to be a Scarborough or Cambridge United supporter, but rotten if you happen to love the game for its own sake.

A couple of seasons ago I went to see Fulham play Chelsea, and as I remember the scoreline was 5-3. The ball was flying from one end of the field to the other, the crowd was going crazy, particularly the Chelsea fans who thought it was fabulous. I was sitting next to Terry Venables and I thought he was reading my mind when he turned to me at the end and said: 'Is it my imagination or was that a bad game?'

I said: 'I thought it was a bad game, too.'

Terry, who is a manager I have a lot of admiration for, said: 'I didn't like to say anything just in case it was me.'

But that's English football today: all kick and rush. That's why I say thank goodness for Liverpool. They know that they have eleven players on the park, whereas most of the First Division sides play as if they have only eight. They boot the ball and rush after it. They might as well leave their midfield men on the bench for all the work they're allowed to do.

kicked off will have given the ball away; and I'm almost always right. A player kicks off. He passes it to the player beside him. He kicks the ball upfield and a charge of lunatics goes rushing after it. It goes out of play. Where's the skill? Where's the entertainment? Football, after all, is simply a form of showbusiness, and there's little entertainment in watching 20 outfield players rushing around like the proverbial headless chickens.

All you hear managers talk about today is graft and work rate. Flair and charisma are rarely mentioned. Skill is almost a dirty word. Individuality is outlawed. And people wonder why we're falling further and further behind the rest of the world in a sport which we invented.

I'm not in a position to reverse this trend but when I coach young children I do what I can. I tell them: be yourself, be individual. The best age to get this across to them is when they are between eight and ten, before they have that innocent, untutored flair knocked out of them. And I tell them: enjoy yourself. Football should not be a chore, it should be a pleasure, which is why we all started playing the game in the first place. Of course they have to work hard at their skills but that shouldn't take the excitement out of it. It comes down to the challenge. When I was young I would practise bouncing the ball up, on my foot without it touching the ground. If I could do it ten times I would try and do it 11 times the next day. Kids are no different today. They rise to the challenge and they want to get better and better. They want to do better than their friends, and by the end of the week you have got a dozen of them capable of keeping the ball in the air for over 20 bounces at a time.

With older boys the same principles still apply but by that stage the coaching has to become a little more specialised. When I was playing, Sir Matt Busby would work with us individually. Take Denis Law, for instance. Denis was not the type of player who enjoyed going on ten-mile runs. Some players, players who were not as gifted as Denis, were dependent on fitness and strength. That was their contribution to the game. Denis's greatest asset was the sharpness of his feet, so you worked on that. Denis was deadly in the penalty box. He had an uncanny ability to take advantage of half-chances, so you developed that aspect of his game. He wasn't made to

The "King" and I. With Dennis Law before a training session. Even training was fun in those glory days. (© Beta Colour Services)

deadly in the penalty box. He had an uncanny ability to take advantage of half-chances, so you developed that aspect of his game. He wasn't made to run back and kick balls off his own goal line, as players are expected to do today. He was there to score goals – and he scored 20 or 30 a season.

In my case the aspect of my game that we continued to work – apart from ball control which I always loved practising – was speed over short distances. I was constantly working to improve my sharpness over ten to 15 yards. And not just sprinting forwards, but backwards too. I used to run backwards against the other players in training. I would get them facing the right way on a line and I would get a little start; they would not start until I moved. At my best there were very few players who could catch me over 20 yards and the advantage that gives you in a game is immeasurable.

This attention to such individual details is vital in sport. It is the way it works in American football where the defence has its own coach, because defence is a specialist skill, and the offence has its own coach. Even the kickers have their own coach. It is the same in baseball. They work on individual aspects because individuality, I emphasise, is vital in sport.

I read sometimes of managers telling players to get their hair cut. I know it sounds like a silly thing – and I am not suggesting that any player should turn up to a match dressed like a tramp – but it worries me when I see a team arrive for the Cup Final and all 15 players are wearing the same ties and the same shirts and the same suits. They are obviously being told how to dress and that annoys me because what else are they being told to do? Can you imagine telling Ruud Gullit to get his hair cut? Or me in my playing days? If you enforce that kind of discipline off the field it will show on the field too. As a lot of great teams have shown, you can accommodate outstanding individuals without detracting in any way from the team performance. And who would you rather have in your side: Ruud Gullit, dreadlocks and all, or neat, well-turned out, well-groomed Neil Webb?

When I coached the Malaysian National Youth Team I didn't tell them how to dress or how to cut their hair. All I was interested in was how they played and how I could improve them. I watched them in training a couple of times before I took over. They were working on shooting exercises and the number of them who could not hit a target made me wonder if I was looking at the future England team. Everyone wanted to break the back of the net, everyone wanted to hit the ball at a hundred miles an hour but all that was happening was that the balls were screaming wide or yards over the bar. It was like some idiotic competition designed to see not who could score a goal, but who could hit the ball the hardest.

On the first day I told them that everyone likes scoring goals but you don't have to rip the net in half to do so. All you have to do is put the ball over the white line. That is the Jimmy Greaves theory. They reckon that half of Greavsie's goals never hit the net. But they did cross the line, and that's all that counts. So we worked on that for a couple of days and we worked on their ball skills and eventually it started to get through. At the end of the week we played the full national side and the result was very rewarding for me.

I was playing for the youth side and I put one of my kids clear with a pass. He went towards the goalkeeper and I could see him steadying himself to blast it. Then, as the keeper moved off his line about ten yards the kid remembered what I had taught him. Instead of smashing it he chipped the ball over the keeper with all the finesse of a Jimmy Greaves or a van Basten. The same thing happened ten minutes later. Another lad got the ball, dummied the keeper, took it round him, and neatly tapped it in just as I had shown him how to do in training. In the end we beat the national side four goals to two. My lads thought that was marvellous. So did I. The local press thought I was some sort of Messiah. That's the joy of coaching. You can see your ideas put into practice, and that's very rewarding.

It's especially true with a youngster. You see an almost instant improvement at that age. You can impress on them the need for skill and get them to work at it and within a couple of hours you can see results. They are also very easy to inspire. Pele called football the beautiful game, and when you look at the skills the Brazilians possess you can see exactly what he meant. My style of play was sometimes compared to the Brazilians and I took that as the highest compliment. They may have gone off the boil compared to

47

what they used to be – but then how many times can you produce players of the quality of Pele or Garrincha? When the Brazilians played it was like I had blinkers on. I would drop everything – the booze, the girls – to watch them on television.

When I was a youngster I went to Sheffield to see Sheffield Wednesday play Santos. Pele was playing and I was dazzled. He took a penalty and I can still see him in my imagination. He moved his hips and pretended he was going to shoot. The keeper moved but Pele didn't kick the ball. The keeper got ready again and Pele went to take it again and then didn't. He must have sent the keeper lurching the wrong way four times and by the time he did take it the poor keeper didn't know whether he was coming or going.

The authorities have stopped that now. These days you have got to move forward and take the penalty in one fluid motion. Back in the early 1960s, however, you could get away with little tricks like that and after I saw Pele do it I went away and practised it myself. It was another skill in the repertoire. But that, of course, is the Brazilian way. They're always looking for new ways of doing things. They live soccer as a dream. They want to do things differently. They want to score goals the way the people on the terrace fantasise about scoring them.

That's the way I played football. In the 1970 World Cup Pele tried to lob the goalkeeper from inside his own half. He missed by no more than a yard. I'd tried to do that. After I saw Pele attempt it I tried even harder. He knew what I was doing and I knew what he was doing and it became like a gentlemanly competition to see who could do it first. Every time we kicked off I would look up and see if the goalkeeper was off his line. And if the lob was on I would go for it.

Unfortunately, most goalkeepers quickly worked out what I was up to and I never managed it. But then neither did Pele. That didn't stop us trying, however. When we were both playing in the United States we were forever trying to guide the ball over goalkeepers' heads from 50, 60 yards. But we were always a tantalising couple of feet wide or the goalkeeper would manage to scramble back and turn the ball away.

It has to be possible, though. You have just got to hit

Me with the second best player in the world – Pele.

the ball correctly. Someone, some day will do it. But not, I fear, any British player. They haven't got the footballing intelligence to try it. I doubt if there are more than a handful of players in the country who have the skill even to hit the target from inside the box. I see players earning anything up to £3000 a week who can't even pass a ball 20 yards. I'm not talking about pin-point passes of 30 or 40 yards which are the sign of true greatness. I'm talking about simple bread and butter passes which the fans have every right to expect – it is the fans, after all, who are paying the wages of these clowns.

Paul Gascoigne of Spurs is an exception. He is accused of being arrogant, unable to cope with the press and liking a drink – which, to me, sounds like he has a chance. He also tries to entertain, which is something very few players seem to want to do any more. And he tries to do things with the ball other than kick it as far as possible up the field.

I was the same. I was always trying to score directly from a corner. It was like playing golf; always competing against yourself. I did it once against Ipswich at Old Trafford in a League match. Bobby Robson, now of England, was the manager of Ipswich then and he said it was a fluke – which shows you how much he knows about football.

United were playing Ipswich again the following week in the F.A. Cup, and I decided that since Robson had said it was impossible to score directly from a corner, I was going to score from the first corner we got. I nearly did. I floated it in, just the way Jimmy Greaves used to, aiming for a spot right under the bar. Unfortunately the ball hit the far post and instead of turning in, it bounced out. But it was close, as close as you could get, and I had made my point, although I'm not certain that Robson ever really understood what was going on.

Another thing I was always trying to do was score from the kick-off. The first time I did that was when I was playing for the juniors at Manchester United. The game was against a Blackburn B side and the score was 0-0 at half time. When we came back on the field John Fitzpatrick, who later went on to play in the Youth Cup-winning team and the first eleven, said he was going to give me the ball directly from kick-off.

'Go on Bestie,' he said, 'go and score and get this game over with.'

There were about three inches of snow on the ground that day. We should never have been playing, and if it had been a First Division game it would have been postponed. But this was just a junior fixture and the managers decided to get it out of the way. Which is all we wanted to do – it was freezing out there on the training ground where we were playing.

Fitzy kicked off and gave me the ball, just like he said he would. I set off and ran straight through the Blackburn team and scored. I turned to Fitzy and said, 'Was that what you wanted?' He said, 'That's exactly what I wanted.'

It felt good. It must have looked good to the ten spectators. And as far as I am concerned, it's moments like that that make a game of football worth the price of admission.

You can't train for it. All you can do is work on your skills and then go out and use them – spontaneously, when the opportunity arises. Most of the time you do not even think about it, like the time we were playing against Spurs and big Pat Jennings, the goalkeeper, punched the ball down and it came to me. There were three or four defenders between me and the goal. I had five or six options. I could have brought it down. I could have controlled it. I could have passed it to someone or I could have set off and tried to wriggle my way through the defence. I did none of these things. In that split second I decided to lob it over everybody. And it worked.

Another time we were playing Chelsea. I had the ball and the Chelsea keeper, Peter Bonetti, had come off his line and pushed me right out towards the corner flag. When he had pushed me wide he turned and started to run back to his goal, which was the correct thing to do. I spun round and saw Denis Law in the middle of the penalty box, alone and unmarked. I thought of passing the ball to him which is what I should have done. But I'd done all the hard work, I'd created the opening and I decided that Denis was not going to get the ball, that I was going to score – and from a near impossible angle on the goal line. I should never have tried it. But vanity comes into the equation at moments like that and instead of playing the ball across to Denis and letting him tap it home, I played it off the inside of my foot and curled it into the net.

When things like that came off I got a huge charge of adrenalin; and it was adrenalin that gave me the rush to score what I consider was my greatest goal. I was playing in the United States for San José. It was 1980, and not a good time for me. I was drinking too much. I had problems with the injury to my right leg. I was getting into trouble with the referees every week. And the referees in America at that time were a joke. They didn't know the rules properly. They didn't understand the difference between a fair challenge and a professional foul, and the man in charge of that game was worse than most.

I had been kicked all afternoon. After I had been tripped for the umpteenth time the referee finally awarded our side a free kick. The player delegated to take the kick was lining up for a shot but I was so angry with the way things had been going I said, no, give the ball to me. I knew what I was going to do. I was going to score. He tapped the ball and said: 'Have your shot.'

That was the start of it. I just decided that they were not going to get the ball off me. I set off. I beat one player, then another. By the end I had beaten five of them in the space of ten yards. I didn't know how I did it and still don't. When I see it on television it still dazzles me.

The fascinating thing about that goal is that while I was scoring it the world went into slow motion. Apparently the same sort of thing happens to racing drivers. When they first accelerate the road starts becoming narrower and narrower. Then, as the brain starts working faster and faster in order to deal with the increasing speed, the road appears to widen out again. And even though they're approaching the corners at ever-increasing speeds, they actually feel as if they are coming up slower.

That's what happened to me. I felt as though I had all the time in the world. One player would come at me but I could see him coming. Then another would come in, but I could see him coming too. And those players were no fools. Cubillas, the Peruvian international, was in their side. They had a lad called Kenny Fogerty who had played for Stockport, Ray Hudson who had played for Newcastle and a Chilean centre half who knew how to get stuck in. But they couldn't get near me. For that moment I was on a different level. The whole sequence, from the moment I got the ball through to the moment I put it into the net, can't have taken more than ten seconds. When it happened I could have sworn it took ten times longer. It was as if time was standing still. When I watch it in slow motion on television it's like watching it the way it happened.

That's what my talent let me do – it let me live the dream of every boy and man in the world.

Chapter Four

Hard Men

THERE WAS AN Arsenal defender named Peter Storey who played 17 times for England, though goodness knows why he was ever selected to play for his country. Every time I played against him he would tell me, before the kick-off, that he was going to break my leg, and worse. I used to look forward to my confrontations with Storey and men like him. I used to love it when players said they were going to do that to me. At the first opportunity I got I would run straight at them and slip the ball through their legs and run around them. Sometimes I would then bring the ball back and do it again. I took particular pleasure in turning Storey inside out and leaving him on his backside: in other words, humiliating him.

On other occasions I would stand on the ball and invite them to come and get it off me, like a matador inviting the bull to charge. Call it mickey taking, call it showmanship, call it stupid, call it whatever you want – but it proved who was the better player, and that was the point. You're not going to invite someone to come and kick you if you can't get out of the way before they do, and I could. It was fun. And it gave me an enormous psychological advantage in a game.

I had nothing but contempt for the so-called hard men. For hard men I always read, men who couldn't play. Because if you do have the skills, the real talent, you're not going to squander them in spending the afternoon trying to kick an opponent. You're going to play football. That's why I always made it a point to try and stick the ball through the legs of my markers the first time they came in and tried to tackle me. I did it against Ron Harris of Chelsea, Paul Reaney of Leeds and Liverpool's Tommy Smith, though it was danger-ous trying it against Smithy – it used to aggravate him and made him more determined to kick you into the stands – but I still always tried it.

In a way they made it easy for me. I always knew that

Harris and Smith and Reaney, or Reaney's team mate Norman Hunter, were going to be snapping around my legs during a game. I knew they were going to be climbing all over me. And because I knew where they were – I could hear them, I could smell them – it gave me an advantage. I was always expecting them to come in on me – and if you're expecting it you can get away from it.

Against Leeds United I had to be on my guard for the whole game. They were a terrible side to play. They were always niggling and complaining to the referee and 'giving you the verbal', which means questioning the sexual behaviour of your mother, your legitimacy, the mental health of your children. They would say anything to provoke you. And they were dirty. Leeds was the only team I ever wore shinguards against. And they had Paul Reaney. Reaney was the toughest player I played against. He was at you the whole 90 minutes, using every dodgy trick in the book.

It was a shame because Reaney did not have to play like that. He had a lot of talent. He was capable of playing good football. He chose instead to subvert his talent. But that was the way Leeds played under Don Revie. And that's why, no matter how many Cups or Championships they won, nobody liked them. The fans on the terraces could see what they were up to and they hated them for it.

The Manchester United team I played in could also look after itself, of course. We had Paddy Crerand. And we had Nobby Stiles. He was the man the other fans came to boo. It was Nobby's style. He had a reputation for being hard but it was the way he played that made him hard to get the better of. He would be assigned on specific occasions to do a specific job and he did it better than anybody I have seen. We rarely marked man for man, but if we played a team like Benfica and Eusebio was playing it was Nobby's job to stop him.

He was once assigned the task of stopping me. It was in an England-Northern Ireland game at Wembley. Nobby came up to me before the start and said, 'Sorry Bestie, I've got to stick to you. I've been told not to leave your side.'

I said, 'Fine, that's your job – let's see who wins.' He was very difficult and it's debatable who came out on top.

I scored. But they beat us 2-1. And I had Stiles on my back the whole game.

He didn't take any prisoners but he was more awkward than malicious. He was niggly, like a terrier, always at your heels. You couldn't knock him away. And if you did get past him he came right on after you. He also couldn't see. He was as blind as a bat. He wore contact lenses but he kept losing them, they kept falling out, and he spent almost as much time looking for his lenses as he did looking for me. That made it harder, not easier, because, without his lenses he wasn't able to judge distances properly and he kept clattering into me.

It wasn't the defenders, however, who caused the real problems. It was the forwards. Players like Chelsea's Peter Osgood, Southampton's Terry Paine, Mike Summerbee of Manchester City and, most especially, Johnny Giles of Leeds. They were hard. But they also had skill which enabled them to get away with subtle fouls that the referee couldn't spot.

When I was playing the fans used to wince at the sliding tackles from the back and they are banned now. But it was never the tackles from the back that damaged you. You might end the game with a few bruises on the back of your legs but it was rare to suffer any worse damage because it's actually very difficult deliberately to break a bone with a tackle. With a back tackle it's almost impossible because your momentum carries you forward, so cushioning the impact.

A tackle from the front is a different matter and the forward players were masters at it.

I was once caught by Johnny Giles, and it could have ended my career. At the start of the game he said to me, 'Why can't you be like Bobby Charlton? He's a gentleman.' I ignored that. Those kinds of remarks didn't bother me. Then, about an hour into the game, he came in over the top. An over-the-top tackle is when a player brings his boot down on the shin bone of his opponent. When done at speed and with enough pressure applied the shin bone breaks.

The tackle, needless to say, is completely illegal.

Because we were playing Leeds I was wearing shinguards. If I hadn't been wearing them my leg would most probably have been broken. As it was, Giles' studs tore through my sock, split the shinguard and cut my leg open. And then Giles had the nerve to say to me again: 'Why can't you be more like Bobby Charlton?'

I was hurt. But I wasn't going to stay down. I wasn't going to let him know that he had hurt me. That would have been belittling myself. The way I played made soccer like a combat sport and I certainly wasn't going to let my opponents know that they had harmed me. And they only rarely did. Instead I raised my performance to meet the challenge. I used to love playing against teams like Chelsea, Liverpool and even Leeds, teams with recognised hard men, because I usually played well against them.

I didn't mind people trying to kick me, trying to have a go at me. I accepted that as part of the confrontation. And I was quite capable of looking after myself. One of the nicest things Sir Matt ever said to me was that I was the best tackler at the club. I certainly never regarded myself as a dirty player, however. I broke two players' legs, but in all honesty I never set out to hurt either of them.

Both incidents were almost exactly the same as each other, with two players sliding in face-on for 50-50 balls. One involved Glyn Pardoe of Manchester City, the other Ian Evans of Crystal Palace, and if anyone was at fault I think they were because their challenges were just a fraction late. When we collided I could hear the bones in their legs crack – as soon as we connected I knew their legs were broken.

I felt utterly sick. I didn't want to play on. If I could have come off I would have. It was a dreadful feeling and I spent the rest of both games just going through the motions. There was absolutely no malice or forethought on either occasion. There's a difference between sliding in to tackle and going over the top. If you go over the top to try and break somebody's leg you have one foot firmly on the ground to provide the leverage when you bring the other one stamping down. You are not skidding across the turf on your backside like I was.

Only once did I deliberately set out to try and hurt someone and that was years later in a charity game for a little amateur club in Belfast. Their gates had averaged two hundred. When I played about five thousand turned up to watch.

The manager told me: 'There's a lad playing on the other side who says he's going to kick you.'

I replied: 'If he wants to kick me he will.'

It didn't worry me. I'd spent my professional career playing against players like Smith, Harris, Reaney, and Dave McKay of Spurs, who was unquestionably the hardest man I ever played against and certainly the bravest – he broke his own leg three times and each time he made it back into the First Division. This time it was just a cocky kid with ideas above his station. He was as good as his word, however. He followed me everywhere. He kicked me and he kicked me again. I told him: 'This is ridiculous, this is an exhibition game. It should be fun.'

He kept on kicking and he started insulting me. All the usual stuff like, 'You're past it, you're a has-been, you won't finish the game.'

I said, 'If you kick me again, *you* won't finish the game.' He did. So about ten minutes later I deliberately knocked the ball a little too far forward, or so he would think, knowing he was going to come in for it. And when he did I turned him and hit him above the knee. As they carried him off, he was crying like a kid. While he was lying on the ground the captain of our team went over to him and said, 'Kittens don't fuck cats.'

I felt very upset about it afterwards. I went to see him after the game to apologise. His manager said, 'Don't worry, George, it's taught him a lesson – don't fuck with a truck.'

Truck is not a word I would ever have used to describe myself. I was always the puny one, slighter than the men employed to mark me. I was one of those players who very rarely got badly injured, however. I spoke to a sports therapist in America about this. We were talking about injuries and he said that he was amazed at the poor balance of so many of the supposedly top sportsmen he saw. His theory was that too many athletes don't know how to fall properly, that they fall awkwardly. The secret, the therapist explained, is to relax. When my son Calum was a baby he jumped out of my arms one day and dropped onto his head on a concrete floor. If he had been a grown-up he would have severely injured himself. Because he was a baby he didn't. He didn't even seem to notice what had happened.

At the peak of my career I feint to the left, go right and another one bites the dust. (© Bob Thomas)

It's this ability to relax like a baby at the point of impact that the therapist was trying to teach the athletes who came to see him. It was almost like a judo course. He had them in the gymnasium, showing them how to fall, how to break the fall, how to relax. This doesn't stop a player going in as hard as he wants. I always went in hard. It was, the sports therapist elaborated, all a matter of balance. And the one thing I always had was balance. I could ride a tackle. Even when they did catch me I didn't fall awkwardly because I was relaxed. My balance was right.

That was one reason the so-called hard men weren't able to intimidate me. They couldn't hurt me in any serious, long-term way – the injuries I picked up and which still bother me come from the cumulative effect of years of wear and tear. Nor, I must say, were they ever as hard as they liked to think they were, not compared to some of the foreigners I played against. The South Americans and the Italians made an art out of dirty play, with every game a succession of professional fouls.

When you were about to jump for a corner they would

stand on your foot and by the time you had kicked their foot away the ball was gone. Or they would stand really close to you and punch you in the kidneys just as the ball was coming over. The very least that did was take your mind off the game for a moment. But you got to know their tricks and how to deal with them. You learnt that if you stood still they would clobber you so you learnt to keep moving. When you did that the shirt pulling would start, but at least that way you were likely to get the free kick awarded in your favour instead of having it awarded against you for trying to push them away as they were about to punch you in the back. If you did make any contact with them they would instantly fall to the ground. By the time they stopped rolling they would be 20 yards away from where the incident took place.

British players didn't behave like that. If we fell over it was because we'd been knocked over and we always tried to get up again as quickly as possible. But when you were playing foreign opposition, even looking to avoid incidents didn't stop them developing. In a match at Old Trafford against the Yugoslavian side Sarajevo I fell over in the penalty area trying to go for a cross. The ball ran out of play and their keeper came across to help me back onto my feet – or so I thought. But as he started to lift me he started digging his nails into my back. I swung out with the back of my hand, which may have looked as if I was being ungracious but was really no more than irritation combined with self-protection.

That was the start of it. For the rest of the match, whenever I went near the 'keeper, he would wag his finger at me and say in broken English, 'You, after the game.' I told Paddy Crerand that the keeper was going to get hold of me the moment the final whistle blew. Paddy told me I was being stupid. I wasn't. When the game was finished and we were walking down the players' tunnel the goalkeeper moved to get hold of me. Paddy stepped in and tried to get hold of him. The next moment everyone was involved. Fists and boots were flying, everyone was shouting, people were wrestling with each other. The fight carried on right up the tunnel, almost into the dressing rooms.

We were told afterwards that poor old Sir Matt had caught a stray blow. He had been up in his seat in the directors' box and had no idea what was going on down below. By the time he made his way to the tunnel most of the players had cleared off into the dressing rooms. But there were still a few milling around, and when he opened the sliding door that leads into the tunnel and put his head around somebody smacked him in the mouth. But at least that was a red-blooded, masculine confrontation, and although it was hardly an advert for football, players accept that such incidents do happen.

What the Argentinians did was a different matter altogether. Sir Alf Ramsey was right. They were animals. I didn't mind anyone taking a swing at me. After all, I could always push them back. That was not the way the Argentinians set about upsetting you, however. They used to come up and spit in your face, time and time again. It's very difficult not to react to that. If someone tackles you and it's a bad tackle you just get up and forget about it. When someone walks over to you and spits in your face while the ball is 50 yards away and the linesmen and the referee are unsighted, it's very hard to resist the instinct to do something about it, especially when it has happened three or four times. What you don't want to do is turn the other cheek.

I was never sent off for kicking anybody. I was sent off for arguing with incompetent referees. I was once sent off for swearing at one of my own team mates. More often I was sent off for losing my temper in retaliation – which, of course, is exactly what an opponent is trying to achieve when he spits in your face or digs his nails into your back, pulls your hair or calls you a masturbator.

Chapter Five

United Disunited

S UCCESS CAN BE as corrosive as failure; and Manchester United has still not recovered from winning the European Cup.

I was 22 years old when we beat Benfica at Wembley on 29 May, 1968, and became the first English team to claim the greatest prize in club football. For Sir Matt Busby it was the vindication of his life's work. It was Bobby Charlton's personal testimonial to the friends and colleagues he had lost in the Munich disaster. For Bill Foulkes it was the obliteration of a nightmare. Denis Law, who didn't play in the final but had played such a vital role in the campaign to get there, had achieved what Sir Matt had bought him to do; and that victory had provided the final justification, if a player of Law's talent ever needed justifying, for the record-breaking £115,000 it had cost to bring him to Old Trafford.

They'd done it, they were proud and they had every reason to be. And then they sat back and you could almost hear the energy and ambition sighing out of the club. It was not that the willingness to win had disappeared completely. It was still there. But after the European Cup it didn't seem quite so important. It was like being in at the winding up of a company.

That was not the way I wanted it. The others were coming to the end of their careers. I was still in the middle of mine. I wanted to win things – I was hungry for more success and that night at Wembley should have provided the foundation for a decade of glory, the way it did for Liverpool when they repeated our achievement and won the European Cup. It didn't. Six years later United, the most famous club in the world, went down into the Second Division. By then I had had enough.

It might have been different if we'd been successful in 1966. I'm certain we would have beaten Real Madrid in the final. And if we had Sir Matt would have started rebuilding his team earlier, at the right time, before it started crumbling away with old age. He might even have retired and let a new manager shoulder the unpleasant responsibility of cutting out the ageing wood. That isn't what happened. We were knocked out by Partizan Belgrade. Sir Matt decided to carry on and take another run at the trophy that had always eluded him. And, rather than bringing in fresh blood, he decided to stick with the players he had. Between 1964 and 1968 he only bought one player, the goalkeeper Alex Stepney. Out of sentiment he hung on to players much longer than he should have done.

It's hard to break up a great team, especially one that had served him so well. But it has to be done and the one club that has done so consistently and brilliantly is Liverpool – and look at the success they've enjoyed. At United we just muddled along with players who were just about to retire or thinking about retiring or should have been thinking about retiring. But the tide of age cannot be turned back and when the inevitable could not be put off any more it was not just one or two players who needed replacing – it was virtually the whole team.

In previous years United had depended on youngsters coming up through the ranks, supplemented with one or two expensive imports of which Law is the best example. But the supply of youngsters had started to dry up; United has not won the Youth Cup since I played in the youth team in 1964 which, for a club of its size, is inexcusable. That meant resorting to the cheque book and that proved to be a disaster. United was always able to breed great players. It has proved over and over again that it doesn't know how to buy them; and some of the players it purchased were a disgrace to the red jerseys they wore.

It was not as if there were no good players available. In those days everyone wanted to play for United. Alan Ball was leaving Blackpool and he let me and everyone else know that he wanted to move to Old Trafford. He even said so in the newspapers. The Blackburn centre-half Mike England was the same. He was also on the move and he too wanted to sign for us. Neither of them did. Ball went to Everton, Mike England joined Spurs. Instead we got players like Willie Morgan from Burnley and Ian Ure from Arsenal. Ure was well past his peak – and I never thought that Morgan was a good player. He was competent on the ball, and could beat opponents with ease, with almost as much ease as I could. But once he had gone past them he didn't know what to do with the ball. He was certainly not a player who was going to help a team win championships.

But by the end of the 60s I think the boss had had enough. I wouldn't say that Sir Matt had lost interest. It was just that he had achieved it all; he'd won everything he'd set out to win. He was getting older, and football didn't hold the same excitement any more. I felt the same, though in my case it was not because I had achieved everything but because I was not likely to achieve anything more, the way things were going. Whereas previously I never believed that anybody could beat us, it quickly got to the stage when I was worrying about going out onto the park because I knew that sooner or later some good team like Leeds was going to give us a thrashing.

I went to see Sir Matt and told him that he should make me captain. Law, Crerand and Charlton were on their way out, the team was clearly in need of rebuilding and I told him that it should be rebuilt around me. I wasn't being arrogant. I was being sensible. It is what the Dutch did with Johann Cruyff. It is what the Argentinians did, more recently, with Maradona.

Sir Matt said: 'You're not responsible.'

I said: 'Make me captain and I will be responsible.'

What I was saying was hard for Sir Matt to accept. He had been in the business for 40 years and here was a 22-year-old basically telling him how to run his club. If you asked him now I'm sure he would say that I was right. Then he just said no and it became an exercise in role fulfilment. I always gave my best on the field, no matter what I thought about the quality of the players I was asked to play with. I never let United down when I played. But because I was being treated as if I was irresponsible I started behaving irresponsibly off the park. I became a rebel, especially when we carried on buying bad players and playing bad players and passing over the good players who were available. The bad players started making me look bad, and that made me worse.

There was another reason for my growing disillusionment. I discovered that both Charlton and Law were still earning a lot more than me. The money was never that high on my list of priorities. I would much rather win games with a club than take money off it, and it was not as if I was exactly running short – my earnings off the field were much greater than anything United paid me. That said, your salary is a measure of your worth. By that stage I was on £700 a week. Which was fine until I discovered that both Law and Charlton were earning twice that – and Law was in the reserves. I said to Sir Matt: 'I've been the leading scorer for six years and I don't think anybody at this club should be getting more money than me.' Sir Matt said, yes, he would look into it. He didn't. Nothing was done about it. I felt as if I was banging my head against a brick wall.

If things were bad at the club they were worse away from it. My life was going insane. I started getting into bother when I went out. There was always some rival supporter or some drunk who wanted to show what a man he was by trying to take on George Best. The press were following me everywhere and everything I did, however trivial, was elevated to front-page news. If I went out with a girl I was supposed to be getting married. If I stopped going out with her I was accused of dumping her. Sir Matt went so far as to suggest that I should take a wife. He said: 'You've got to get married, that'll quieten you down.' That led directly to the ludicrous situation involving Eva Haraldsted.

We went on tour to Denmark shortly after I had that talk with Sir Matt. A girl came to the hotel we were staying at and asked me for an autograph for her boyfriend. She was very pretty with a lovely figure, and when we got back to Manchester I asked the local newspaper to help me find her. They did, and she came over to England – without her boyfriend – and I installed her in the little hideaway flat I had rented with Manchester City's Mike Summerbee. A week later we were engaged.

Sir Matt was furious. He called me back into his office and asked me what I thought I was doing. I said: 'I'm getting married – you told me to get married.'

He protested: 'You can't get married, you only met her a week ago.'

He was right, of course, and a short while later I got fed up with her, decided that the whole thing was a nonsense, and called the whole thing off. Eva had learned quickly, however. She sued me in what must be the last case of its kind before the law was changed, for breach of promise and collected £500 off me. She didn't go away, though. She hung around Manchester and kept turning up at Blinkers, the night club I went to. I got annoyed at this and one night I went into the disc jockey's booth and put the Beatles' record, 'Get Back', on the turntable. And I put it on over and over again.

The man she was with, a big fellow who stood well over six feet, took exception. Paddy Crerand, who was in the club with me, took exception to his taking exception and Paddy, the guy and his brother ended up brawling outside on the pavement. Paddy ended up in court where he was cleared of all charges.

United were very protective of their own in those situations. They gave you all the help they could. Football was a religion to Sir Matt and he took a personal interest in the welfare of his players. By this time I had become a regular visitor to his office where he would sit me down and ask me what was wrong and said he would do anything he could to help – the captaincy and a pay rise excepted.

There was nothing anyone could do, however. The problems were mine and they were getting worse.

I moved out of my digs with Mrs Fullaway and into this futuristic house I had built for myself in Bramhall in Cheshire. When I moved in I thought: 'This is great. You are earning a fortune. You are driving around in a brand new E-type. Now you've got a home with an ornamental pool and table tennis and a snooker table and you can have all your friends around on Sunday for lunch and a game of snooker.'

That, at least, was the idea. It turned into a nightmare. My friends did come round for lunch, just as I'd planned. But so too did thousands of tourists. On Sundays coach loads of sightseers would arrive to ring my front doorbell and picnic in my garden and let their kids steal the goldfish from the pond. It got so bad that I was afraid to answer the door or go near the windows.

The house itself was a horror. Everything was push-button. The bathroom had a sunken bath that was so large that the water tanks couldn't fill it higher than three inches. I had

The Striking Viking, Eva Haraldsted. An engagement I didn't keep.
(© Camera Press)

a television set that disappeared into the chimney. I had a console beside the bed that controlled everything. All I had to do was press a button and I could open and close the garage door, the front door, operate the television and the stereo, open and close the curtains. Which was all well and good until I found out that when an aeroplane flew overhead, it set off the whole system.

It happened one night and it was like a scene from Monty Python. I was looking after an eight-month-old red setter and when I came home one night I found the poor little dog cowering in the corner. I had closed the garage door before I left. It was open when I got back so I thought there might be an intruder in the house. I searched all the rooms and then went back and tried to stroke the dog. It tried to bite my hand off. So I let him be, made myself a cup of coffee and got into bed. All of a sudden a plane passed overhead and the house went crazy. The TV was going on and off and up and down the chimney, the curtains were opening and closing, the front door was banging and the garage door was going up and down. It was like being in a mad house. The dog went into hysterics again; and I nearly did too. I couldn't even get away from the place without a police escort to clear a path through the rubber-neckers and the press men who were always camped outside. It was like being a prisoner.

By now I had started drinking heavily. Not to the extent I would later. It was not out of control; I was still in my early twenties and I could handle my hangovers. I could get out of bed in the morning and do my full training and not feel the worse for it. The trouble was, however, that I no longer wanted to. I had always loved training and being fit. I loved practising with the ball and testing myself against the other players. Now I started thinking: 'Is it worth it?' And the answer, increasingly, was, 'No, it's not.'

The team was bad and getting worse. It got so bad that I didn't want to wake up in the mornings. And I stopped reading the newspapers. Before I couldn't wait to read them because I knew they would be full of the good things I had done, the good footballing things. But now we were losing and I felt this terrible emptiness.

It was not only me who was upset by this. Charlton was too. We were plying our talents in a wasteland. I felt that no matter what I produced there was no end product. Bobby felt the same and neither of us were very tolerant of the lesser players. We would shout at them, urge them on and try and get them to do the things we believed Manchester United players should be able to do. It didn't work – you can't make a good player out of a bad player, and some of the people we were being asked to play alongside should never have been allowed to wear a Manchester United shirt.

There were some false dawns. In the season after Wilf McGuinness had come and gone and Frank O'Farrell had been made manager, we actually went five points clear at the top of the table. And I was still scoring regularly. I knocked in 15 League goals in the '69-70 season, 18 the following year and 18 again the season after that.

In 1970 I was suspended for four weeks for knocking the ball out of the referee's hand in a fit of temper. My first game back was against Northampton in the F.A. Cup and I scored six. It was real *Roy of the Rovers* stuff, a moment of pure fantasy.

The trouble was, I was the only United player who was getting onto the scoring sheet with any regularity and no one player can single-handedly support a whole team. I started turning up late for training. Then I started missing it altogether. In 1971 I disappeared and went down to London to hole up for a few days with the actress Sinead Cusack who is now married to the actor Jeremy Irons. I was completely screwed up and I wanted someone to talk to. After that 'George Best goes missing' became a regular front page story.

I was lonely, lonely in my own way. When I disappeared I did not go off with the boys for a holiday or go away with some woman for an exotic holiday. I would jump on a plane and go off on my own to Spain and sit in a bar and get drunk by myself. I didn't know what I wanted. All I knew was that I had to get away – from Manchester United, from the goldfish bowl I was living in. I thought I was taking the easy way out. In fact I was not taking any way out at all because there was no way out – I was George Best, whether I liked it or not, and anywhere I went this creature called George Best, footballer superstar, went with me.

Other players have had to endure this kind of pressure. Pele was recognised everywhere he went. So now are Ruud Gullit and Diego Maradona. But there is a difference between them and me. Pele played in three World Cup-winning Brazilian teams. Maradona won the World Cup with Argentina. Gullit plays for the most successful club side in Europe and one of the most exciting national teams in the world. You can learn to live with success like that. I played for Northern Ireland and they were never going even to qualify for the World Cup.

Playing for Northern Ireland was recreational soccer – there was hardly any pressure on you because you were not really expected to get a result, unlike the Brazilian or the Italian or even the English teams are – and the way Manchester United is. But, as I told my friends, Manchester United, in those dying days of my career there, was heading for the Second Division where I had no intention of playing for them, not then, not when I was right at the peak of my ability.

If United had been winning or had had a chance of winning, my story might have been a different one because I believe I could have coped with anything if I could have enjoyed success like Pele's and Maradona's. That was all I wanted. It was not what I was getting. In all the years I had been with United I had never walked out onto the field believing that we were going to be beaten no matter who we were playing. Then it changed. I started looking at the other team and thinking, 'It's going to be a struggle today,' or 'I don't think we are going to win today.'

That was the most awful feeling – to go out and think you were going to lose or, worse, know that you were going to lose against sides that three or four years earlier United would have demolished. It was dreadful for everyone but it was worse for me because I was the one who always took the jeers from the crowd.

I always had attracted the attention of the boo boys but in the early days it didn't matter, because we were winning, because I knew that at the end of the game I could walk off and say, 'It doesn't matter, you can scream all you want – but we won!' But we weren't winning any more. It was like being in a bad dream. The crowd would be booing and jeering and singing their songs about me and when I woke up at the final whistle we had been hammered 4-0.

The atmosphere in the dressing room after those defeats was like a morgue. No one spoke. Sometimes I would sit there by myself after all the other lads had bathed and gone home, not talking, not doing anything, still in my kit, too depressed to move. After an hour and sometimes two like that I would get up and go out and get completely drunk, sometimes for two or three days in a row. Then I would miss training on Monday mornings and the whole thing became a vicious circle.

While all this was happening on the field, my troubles off it were getting even worse. Even going out for a cup of coffee became an ordeal. Perhaps it was just Manchester. Maybe it was just society in general that was changing. But whereas in the past even supporters of the rival City team would slap me on the back and say, 'Well done' (after they had allowed me to enjoy the wisdom of their opinions, of course), I was now running the risk of getting embroiled in a fight every time I went out. I started hating my life. I started hating the hassle of being me.

People would talk about me in front of me as if I was not there. It was like they were talking about someone else, about someone outside the door. Being the me I was supposed to be was an acting job: I was pretending to be me. I felt as if I was watching a monster on television who looked like me and talked like me but wasn't me at all.

Sir Matt suggested I went to see a psychiatrist. He never actually used the word psychiatrist. What he said was: 'I think you need to go and talk to someone,' but there was no doubting what he meant. He was right, of course. I did need someone to talk to. I couldn't talk to my ex-landlady, Mrs Fullaway; she knew nothing about football or the other complications of my life. I could hardly go and unburden myself to the other players. I tried to talk to Sir Matt, but I always found that very difficult and stilted – I was, I suppose, too much in awe of him.

I did have my friends and some of them are still my friends now. There were the inevitable hangers-on – being around a famous person, even if it's just for one drink or one photograph, is one little way for people to get away from their mundane, boring nine-to-five lives – but the people I saw regularly were good and decent. I resented the criticism they attracted. It was not fair on them and it was an insult to my intelligence. What the press was saying was that I could not differentiate between true friends and sycophants. I could: I knew who was only there to hang on to my shirt tails, to catch a little of my stardust, and who wasn't. Even today, if I was in trouble, I could telephone Malcolm Wagner or one or two of the other lads I used to go around with and know that they would be there to give me all the help they could.

They couldn't help me then, though. What I was going through was well beyond their experience. And Sir Matt's idea of going to see a psychiatrist certainly didn't appeal.

It's not in my character to let things out. I tend to keep my thoughts and worries locked up, which is a problem in itself. I would far rather sit on my own and be depressed than talk to somebody, even to my father. I think, 'I don't want to worry him.' It's stupid and it makes everything more difficult and when it all gets to be too much I explode. The Sinead Cusack incident I've mentioned is a perfect example.

I'd been dropped for missing training yet again. We were playing Chelsea that Saturday and I followed the team down to London. I wanted to talk things over with Sir Matt. But when I got to the hotel in Russell Square where he was staying and saw the cameramen and photographers waiting outside I decided I couldn't face it and told the taxi driver to keep going and drive me to Sinead's flat in Islington.

I'd met her some months earlier in Ireland and we'd got on well. We got on well that weekend. She listened while I talked and she was very understanding in a sweet, Irish way. We made the mistake of going out to dinner. We were spotted and followed and spent the rest of the weekend holed up in her apartment watching the television coverage of the crowds gathered on the street outside and listening to the kids beating on her front door shouting, 'We want George.'

We were besieged and afterwards Arthur Lewis, the MP for West Ham North, asked why it was necessary to waste public money providing me with a police escort to help me break out. I was doing some wondering of my own. I was wondering what the hell was happening to me. I can understand why some rock and film stars choose to shut themselves away from the world and become recluses because I was coming to the end of my psychological tether. I was a mental and emotional mess.

After this the disappearances became a habit. I would struggle on for a while and then something would happen – another bad defeat, a business problem, another fight, another mob scene – and I would snap again and get on an aeroplane and tell myself, 'I'm going to live a beach bum's life in Spain.' I didn't know what I wanted, however. I did not know whether I wanted to stay, go, leave for a little while, or simply vanish. But I knew that after six months of doing my own thing or whatever you want to call it (and some people would call it trying to drink myself into the grave), I could always play football, even if it was not for Manchester United. But I knew that I would always get invited back to United.

I didn't know whether I wanted them or whether I didn't want them but I did know that they wanted me. If my walk-outs were a cry for help then United was always prepared to extend a hand. The club has been accused of being too lenient with me but taking me back did make sound financial and football sense. They obviously had trouble with me – but they couldn't do without me.

I was the best player they had and I drew the crowds. Look-ing at it, there is a comparison between what's happening at United now with Bryan Robson and what happened with me then. Everything concentrates on Robson and making sure he is fit and healthy. They would be better off concentrating on the other ten players it takes to make up a team. It would certainly have helped me if United had taken the spotlight off me a little and did what they should have done, which was put together a decent side. Perhaps they should have kicked me out; and I know that Charlton wasn't very happy with the way they always welcomed me back. But then no business willingly discards its best asset without careful con-sideration, and after a few months of hanging around doing nothing I could usually be persuaded to give it another try.

Maybe they guessed that those early walk-outs were not final; the only time I left and knew for certain that I was not going back was when Tommy Docherty was in charge. Before that there was always the chance that I would settle down and regain my old enthusiasm and United were prepared to take it. The walk-outs did not make for easy comebacks, however. They brought me even more publicity, which is exactly what I didn't want. I would lose fitness and it became harder each time to get myself back into condition. Nor did it help matters that every time I came back there was usually a different manager in charge.

It was a shambles. In the space of two years United had five managers: Busby, Wilf McGuinness, Busby again, Frank O'Farrell, and Tommy Docherty. I felt sorry for Wilf. I really wanted him to do well but he was never going to, not with the players he had. There was a lot of talk at the time of a dressing room rebellion, of some senior players refusing to play for him. That was not the case. It was just that he was young and inexperienced which made it difficult to handle some of us, and after six months they fired him. His only chance of achieving something lay with me. I was still at my peak and I could turn it on in a way other players could only envy. But I'd started going my own way. When the other players went off to the movies I sneaked off to the pub. I was skipping training and just generally being difficult, and one day I let him down on the field, and I still feel bad about that.

It was against Leeds in the semi-final of the F.A. Cup and we were staying in a hotel in Birmingham the night before the match. Wilf, who made it his business to keep an eye on me, used the pass key he had and walked into my room half an hour before we left for the game where he found me with a woman who should have been in her own hotel room with her husband but had been persuaded to take a detour into my bed. He was angry when he saw what I was up to. He said, 'I'll be downstairs in the bar,' and walked out.

I followed him down. He downed a large whisky and said, 'You'd better play well today. You've got to do it for me today.' For the first and only time in my playing life I felt under pressure. I kept thinking, 'Right, I've got to do it today. It's the semi-final of the Cup and you've never played in an F.A. Cup final at Wembley. And you've got to do it for Wilf.'

And what happened? The first time I got the ball I tripped over it and fell flat on my face into the mud. And that was only the beginning. I'm not suggesting that we would have won if I had been on form – but having me tripping over the ball and playing the worst game of my life was not going to improve our chances. And it didn't: Leeds, the one team I detested, went on to beat us 1-0; and that still infuriates me.

But Wilf must take some responsibility for what happened in that match. Part of a manager's job is to send his players out in the right frame of mind and to do that you have to tailor your psychology to suit the individual.

Some years later, when I was playing for Fulham, there was a very similar incident. Bobby Campbell, who is now with Chelsea, was the manager and he decided to lock us up in a hotel the night before one particular game. I checked in and then thought to myself, 'What am I doing in a hotel? – I only live around the corner in Putney.' So I checked myself out and went off to the pub where I settled myself down with two girls I happened to find there.

An hour later Campbell walked in. He said, 'Introduce me – and I'll have a Coke.'

He didn't get angry. Quite the opposite – he took me off to a restaurant where the Fulham chairman, Sir Eric Miller, was dining with his family, and kept me up until four o'clock in the morning. When he eventually dropped me back at the hotel he simply said: 'Right, you've got a good eight hours' sleep left – and you'd better play well tomorrow!' The approach worked: I did.

But that was not Wilf's way. He was under pressure and the tension rubbed off on all of us. United had always been a very relaxed, friendly club where everyone had got on well with everyone else. We always said 'Good morning' to each other, from the cleaning lady and the lad who cut the grass all the way through to the manager and up to the chairman, Louis Edwards. But that started to change. The first-team players stopped talking to the juniors. Then, as the results got worse, the first-team players stopped talking to each other. Cliques started to form.

To try and break them up Wilf, who was worrying that people were nattering about him behind his back, changed our sleeping arrangements at away matches. He ruled that instead of sharing our hotel room with a friend as we were used to – I'd always roomed with David Sadler – we would draw lots to decide who would share with whom. It was a ridiculous idea. I was not very keen on his team talks, either. Whereas Sir Matt had basically told us to go out and get on with it, Wilf insisted on explaining everything with diagrams. And by giving each player a specific role he took away the flow and flexibility that had been the hallmark of our play.

But at least you could talk to Wilf. I could never talk to Frank O'Farrell, who was appointed manager in 1971. He arrived a stranger. He left a stranger. I actually liked him as a man but he wasn't up to the job. He just wasn't qualified to handle the club that, for me, is the greatest in the world. He wasn't hard enough. It was difficult getting two words out of him, never mind the right words at the right time.

On the Michael Parkinson chat show on television one night I talked about women and the way some of them would lyingly say, as they started to take their clothes off, 'I'm not doing this because you're George Best.' I was being humorous, but O'Farrell was not amused. He complained: 'George should realise that it's great for someone like Parkinson that he should go on his show and say things like that. It's great for Parkinson but it's not good for George.' He said that to the newspapers. He didn't say anything to me. He never mentioned it. And when I decided that I had to say something about the way things were going on the playing side, I said it to Busby and Edwards, not to him.

What I've never been able to understand is why, with all the money the club has, it has never gone out and bought a top foreign player. For the amount of money United have squandered over the years on second raters – and I include most of the players Alex Ferguson has bought – they could have got themselves the best players in the world. For what they paid for Phelan and McAllister, neither of whom are ever going to pull in the crowds because they are neither glamorous enough nor talented enough, they could have bought Maradona or Ruud Gullit – and think what that would have done for the club and its attendances. The high wages they would have demanded shouldn't have been an obstacle: they would have been more than covered by the extra people they would have attracted through the turnstiles. At the same time United might have re-established itself as a major force in football, the way A.C. Milan has with Gullit and Naples has with Maradona. Instead they bought players like Gary Birtles, who cost £1,250,000 and was sold two seasons later for £250,000, and Alan Brazil, who never achieved anything at Old Trafford. The £13 million Ferguson has paid out has certainly not bought success.

O'Farrell set the style. In the short time he was at United he spent £585,000, a large sum then, on five players. Of those, only one, the defender Martin Buchan, was worth the money. Wynn Davies was too old, Ian Storey-Moore, even if he could score goals, was terribly injury-prone and was never fit enough to make any major contribution. Anderson, from the Irish club Portadown, was hardly a find and Ted MacDougall was just another bad buy.

I felt the situation was hopeless. When I did play, in between the times when I went missing, I was still giving my best, but I had nothing to work with. I recently turned out in a charity football match. Pat Jennings and Alan Ball were playing. These charity games are supposed to be a bit of fun but you still want to win and everyone takes it seriously. Not all the celebrities taking part are footballers, however, which can lead to problems. I had picked the ball up just past the halfway line, gone round the man marking me, pulled the ball back and looked up to pass. I saw that my nearest team mate was the boxer Dave 'Boy' Green and I thought, 'Oh no, anybody but him. Better not to pass – he'll only trip over the ball.'

That was the way it was at Manchester United at the end. I would be passing the ball to certain players, thinking to myself, 'That's the end of the move.' That's a terrible way to think about your team mates. But it was realistic and most of the time I was right and the move would break down.

In 1972 I went to discuss the situation with Sir Matt and the chairman, 'Champagne' Louis, so-called because when we stayed overnight or went on trips abroad, we always knew which was Louis's room because there were always six empty bottles of champagne outside his door in the morning. It was the worst of times for me. I felt that something was going terribly wrong with the club. I didn't really want to leave and I didn't want to play for anybody else. At the same time I didn't want to be there with the situation as it was.

Looking back and with all the benefit of hindsight, what I should have done, instead of walking out, was to have put in a transfer request and moved elsewhere. I had a chance to go to Chelsea. I could have gone abroad – I got whisper that the big Spanish and Italian clubs were interested in me – and looked for a new challenge. If I had known then what I know now I would have gone like a shot. But at the time I didn't want to play for any other club or in any other country. It was United or nothing for me.

I tried to explain all this, which was not an easy thing for me to do, to Busby and Edwards, a big happy-go-lucky rich man who liked the friendship of Sir Matt. I said that the team was going to struggle and that we needed better players. I said that players like Ball and England had wanted to join United. I didn't go so far as to criticise individual players in our squad. I would never have done that. But I did say that I was having to go out and play with players who were not good enough for Manchester United. Busby said: 'We look at players as they come along and talk to them and then make our decision.' After that there was a lot of nodding. Busby and Edwards sat there nodding as I explained my feelings just as I used to nod when I was called into the manager's office for a telling off. It meant that nothing much was going to change.

O'Farrell was angry about my meeting. He felt that I had gone behind his back, that I was undermining his position. I can understand that, although in fact it was O'Farrell who had asked Busby and Edwards to see me in the first place. And if I was going to speak to anybody I wanted it to be them because, like most of the other players, I found O'Farrell so difficult to communicate with. Speaking to Sir Matt and Edwards didn't make a blind bit of difference, however. The team didn't get any better; and the results got worse.

It might have all been so different if Jock Stein had taken over. He was in charge of Celtic and he was the only other British manager then to have won the European Cup. It would have been difficult for him to leave a club where he had been so successful and take over one that had its own glorious record. At United he would not only have to compete with that record but also try and better it. He certainly had all the right credentials for the job, however.

I met Jock several times and he seemed as close as you could get to Sir Matt on all levels, not only in his love of football but in the way he handled people and the way he wanted to play the game. He would have been a great manager for Manchester United and in 1971 it looked as if he was on his way to us. He had held a meeting with Sir Matt – in the back of a car in a petrol station forecourt near Haydock, as it turned out – and the two men had shaken on the deal that was supposed to bring Jock to Old Trafford. Then, at the last minute, Jock decided not to come and the reason apparently was that he did not want to work under the shadow of Sir Matt who was staying on at the club as a director. Certainly Old Trafford is an intimidating place for an outsider. It broke O'Farrell; and it almost killed McGuinness when they sacked him. He lost his hair almost overnight and he couldn't even talk for a long time afterwards.

Stein was different. He was a big man with as big a name as Sir Matt and a lot of self-confidence. He could have run the club in his own way. Having Sir Matt there wouldn't have been a hindrance; if I'd been Stein I would have been very happy to have someone with Sir Matt's experience to talk to and, if it was needed, to ask advice of. And Sir Matt, I am absolutely certain, was man enough and intelligent enough not to have interfered in any shape or form in the running of the team once he had moved upstairs. But Stein clearly thought differently, and that was bad news for United. If you wanted to be cruel you could say that the best thing Sir Matt could have done would have been to walk away from the club.

Yet how could you expect someone who had given almost his whole life to and almost, at Munich, his actual life for Manchester United to say: 'That's it, I am never going to go to Old Trafford again, I am never again going to watch them play.' You couldn't. And that made it a no-win situation for any manager who moved into the manager's seat (but never his office: Sir Matt kept that for himself).

It was a no-win situation for me, too. I was missing training, getting booked, sent off, suspended, fined and dropped. I was into fights and I was having murders with the alcohol. I was ordered to move in with Paddy Crerand and his wife Noreen but that didn't last long. The first night there Noreen asked me what I had for breakfast. I said cornflakes, toast, bacon and eggs. The next morning I came down to the kitchen and there were two slices of bread, two eggs and a couple of rashers of bacon laid out on the table ready for me to get on with. That diminished the length of my stay dramatically. I thought to myself, 'This is definitely not going to work,' and the next day I moved back home. O'Farrell, in the effort to bring me under control, ordered me out of the Bramhall house and back into digs with Mrs Fullaway but that wasn't going to make any difference, either. I was coming to the end.

I never walk away if someone picks a fight with me but I always back away from a confrontation with someone I love. If I have a fight with a girlfriend I walk out. It was the same with United. I know you shouldn't walk out; I know that you are better off staying and trying to talk it out. But rightly or wrongly – and in my case wrongly – I thought the easy solution was to find the nearest bar and have half a dozen drinks until it didn't matter and then not go home or not go back to the club for two or three days and then go back and try and start all over again. But that's no solution at all. It's probably why most of the women I have been with have left me, and it's why Manchester United and I parted company. I made them leave me, and by doing that I let United down.

I let them down by the way I handled things and by the way I disappeared. At the same time I gave them nine glorious years. I was their leading goalscorer for six years and it will be a long time before anyone equals that. While I was there we won the Youth Cup, the League championship twice and if I hadn't been playing we wouldn't have won the European Cup. I was European and British footballer of the year and, to be quite honest, if it hadn't been for me they would have sunk into the Second Division before they did. There is one school of thought that says that I couldn't handle my genius. Another idea might be that Manchester United couldn't handle it. But either way, I paid any debt I might owe to the club by what I did for them on the field. And if it hadn't been for Tommy Docherty I might even have done more for them.

Chapter Six

Charlton

B OBBY CHARLTON AND I never really hit it off. Some people go so far as to say that we hated each other, that we couldn't even bring ourselves to say hello to each other. That's not true. We were never openly, obviously hostile towards each other, and if we see each other today we always exchange greetings. I don't fall into easy conversation with him, though, the way I do with Denis Law or Paddy Crerand. But then I never did. Not being the best of friends is a little different, however, from being the worst of enemies.

All the same, there has always been an unspoken tension between us. That was partly to do with our different lifestyles, partly it was to do with what was happening out on the field, with Manchester United. From his point of view the way I lived and the way I was behaving off the field was letting the club down. His club. And when you remember what he had been through – the Munich disaster, the loss of so many friends and colleagues – you can understand why Bobby felt so proprietorial about United. To many people Charlton, along with Sir Matt, of course, *was* Manchester United. I'll never forget (or forgive) Johnny Giles after he'd nearly ripped my leg off, turning to me and saying: 'Why can't you be like Bobby?' There was a man who had almost crippled me. And there he was trying to tell me that I was the one who should behave more like a gentleman. Bobby never said anything like that. He never suggested to me that I should be more like him. I don't think he was bothered about whether I was letting myself down but he did think that I should have been a little more responsible. Off the field, that is – no one could ever accuse me of not giving everything I had for the club on the park, and when we were playing Bobby was always amongst the first to run across to congratulate me when I scored, and vice versa.

Away from the game, however, we were two very different types of people. When we finished training Bobby went home to his wife while I would go off for a drink with the lads. Bobby mixed differently. By that I mean that he didn't really mix at all; and if I have a criticism of him it is that he was not one of the boys. After an away game when the coach would stop off at a small hotel somewhere for dinner, Bobby would rather stand and have a drink with the directors than with the other players. It was as though he regarded himself as a member of the upstairs team – and everyone else was downstairs.

That did generate animosity, especially as, at the same time, he appeared to lose his sense of humour. But it didn't bother me particularly. Bobby belonged to a different era. When I got into the first team I was just a teenage kid while he was a very senior player and one of the most famous footballers in Britain. We were living in two different worlds. Then, when I became established, we simply went our separate ways. Bobby's sense of humour failure did irritate some of the other senior players, however, like Shay Brennan and Nobby Stiles; but, to be fair, Bobby didn't have much to laugh at by then. The team that had won the European Cup had started to creak with age and Bobby, like me, was very upset at the way we were sliding down from the pinnacle of our achievement. What I don't think Bobby ever accepted was that by the early 1970s he was part of the problem.

He was never very good in the air and we used to laugh and joke about his tackling, even though that really wasn't Bobby's job; in those days the defenders were the ones who were supposed to kick people and tackle. Forwards were supposed to score goals; and Bobby certainly did that. Jimmy Greaves was a great goal scorer. Bobby Charlton was a scorer of great goals. There were numerous times where a game would be in doubt, where it was evenly balanced, or where it looked as if we were out of it when Bobby would pick up the ball 30 or 40 yards out from goal and, whoosh, it would be all over. And he did that consistently. His passing was no less brilliant. He was like radar, picking you out from half a field away. It was a joy to play with him.

As the years rolled by, however, he became less effective. He never cheated the way some players did. He never tried to disguise the weaknesses that come with age, the way some players did; when you can't get to the ball like you used to

Charlton, Best, Law. The Holy Trinity of Manchester United.
(© Sporting Pictures (UK))

be able to you try and make it look as if you can. I thought the lovely Albert Quixall got away with that for two or three years – and if you're cheating yourself you're cheating the club. Bobby wasn't like that. He gave you his total commitment for the whole of the 90 minutes. Even today, in charity matches, he runs around like an 18-year-old. It's a matter of pride. But when a great player, any player, comes towards the end of his career the timing starts to go. That is sad to see, and I could feel it happening to me when I was playing for Hibernian in Scotland a few years later. By the early 1970s Bobby's passing ability was obviously not what it had been. The radar had gone wonky and the balls were going astray. But Bobby kept on and he shouldn't have done.

I wouldn't have liked to have been the manager to first leave Bobby Charlton out of the team. But that is exactly what the manager should have done. That is exactly what Liverpool have always done. Their players give their best and after they have given it Liverpool says 'Thank you very much', and replaces them. United, conversely, tended to keep their players on when it would have been better for all concerned if they had shaken them by the hand and let them go. That was down to Sir Matt's sentimentality. It was for that reason, I believe, that Bobby was able to play on a little longer than he should have. And because of the way the team was constructed around him that started causing problems on the field – as he became less effective United became less effective.

I represented the future of Manchester United, or should have done. Charlton represented the past. And while I don't think he was ever jealous of me – he had nothing to be jealous of – I got the feeling that he resented that.

There were times when Bobby played as if he had blinkers on. I don't know whether he did it consciously – it might just have been my imagination – but I used to feel that in certain circumstances, when I was in the perfect position and Bobby had the ball, he made a point of not passing to me. I used to say some rather disparaging things about Bobby then. Not on the field, not to his face. After all, I could hardly complain about that because I never liked giving the ball away. I always wanted to do everything myself. But if we were playing cards, and someone played a wrong card I would say things like, 'You're making more mistakes than Bobby Charlton.' I refused to play in his testimonial match because, as I said at the time, it would have been hypocritical. I didn't contradict a story that I had spent an evening in the Brown Bull throwing drinks at his picture on the wall (in fact drinks were thrown over everyone's pictures, mine included, but the 'Best throws beer over Charlton' angle fitted the mood at the time).

I've mellowed since then. I'm a nicer person than I was 15 years ago. And I think Bobby has mellowed as well. He looks more relaxed, more like the old Bobby, the Bobby I first knew. His sense of humour is back, and that's a change for the better. And if Manchester United had any sense they would do what they should have done a long time ago – and make him Chairman. He wouldn't make a good manager. He is too dour and a manager needs to be able to get along with people. But he does command the respect of the general public. He's scrupulously honest. He loves the club – apart from his family United is the greatest love of his life. He also has integrity –

and integrity is what United, after all the turmoil it has been going through, desperately needs.

No club has a God-given right to existence. Look what happened to Wolverhampton Wanderers, the team I supported when I was a boy. They were a great club yet they almost went out of business a few years ago. It is very unlikely that that would ever happen to Manchester United – there are a lot of people with a lot of money who would love to be involved with United. But the Knighton takeover fiasco and the boardroom squabbles have strained the loyalties of even the most devoted supporters and left a foul memory.

Manchester United belongs at the top of world football. It should always be challenging for the highest prizes with all the flair and flamboyance that made it famous. It shouldn't be bringing shame on itself with these boardroom battles. Appointing Bobby Charlton Chairman, even if he had to be draughted into the job, would be the most positive step Manchester United could take to restore the reputation of the greatest club in the world. That done, the club would then have the stability so vital to any serious and consistent assault on the League title. Once that had been achieved we might again see the red shirts of Manchester United sweeping through Europe. Europe is where Manchester United belongs. Europe is Manchester United's destiny. Bobby Charlton, the last of the Busby Babes, is the man to lead it back there.

Chapter Seven

Docherty and Out

TOMMY DOCHERTY IS the funniest, most two-faced, self-obsessed man I have met; and he is the reason I finally, unequivocally, quit Manchester United. Tommy Docherty lied to me and that, to me, makes Tommy Docherty a liar. I came back to Manchester United because of him. I walked out on the club I loved, that had been my family, my life for 11 years, because of Tommy Docherty.

I had run away to Spain earlier in 1972. I came back, not quite in an ambulance, but almost. Marbella had not really worked out as I'd imagined it would. I wasn't so stupid as to think that my problems would simply go away because I was in Spain or Ireland or the United States, but by that stage I had decided that I didn't want to remain in the goldfish bowl that Manchester had become for me. After several months, however, of lying around in the sun and making love to every woman I chanced upon, I was starting to miss my football. I hadn't removed my problem. I'd just moved its location. I still wasn't certain that I wanted to go back but the fates intervened and the decision to leave Spain and return to Britain was taken out of my hands.

I was sitting one evening in a Marbella bar, waiting for it to close so that the owner, my girlfriend Chris, and I could go on and make a night of it, when the pain started. At first I didn't think anything of it. It was a dull ache at the top of my right leg, close to the groin and I thought it was the result of sitting propped up at the bar for the past couple of hours. Then the pain got worse and that worried me. I was always very lucky with injuries and I very rarely got ill and this felt like nothing I'd ever felt before. So instead of going on I said to Chris – she's now married to the footballer Frank Stapleton – that I was going to go back to the hotel.

Usually I won't go near a doctor, no matter what's wrong with me, but this time I decided I really had better get some-one to take a look at me. I got the hotel to telephone for one.

He came, sprayed my leg with anaesthetising atomiser, gave me some antibiotics, and declared that there was nothing wrong with me. I informed him that Spanish doctors don't have the greatest reputation in the world, that I knew that there definitely was something wrong and got myself out on the first flight back to Manchester.

I was in an awful state when we touched down. The sweat was pouring off me, the pain was excruciating and my whole leg had swollen up so much that I couldn't put the shoe back on that I'd taken off on the plane. I'd telephoned my friend Malcolm Wagner from the hotel just before I left and he was at the airport waiting to meet me. He'd brought a doctor with him. As soon as we were in the car the doctor told me to drop my trousers. He took one look, and said, 'Oh dear' or words to that effect, drove me straight to hospital and had me on a drip within 20 minutes of touchdown.

I had a thrombosis. I was very lucky. It could have travelled up the body and if it had, and if it had hit my heart or brain, I would have died. Mine had moved down and had lodged in my calf. They don't know what caused it. The doctors said that it might have been a knock, that I could have bumped myself on a chair, or more likely in my case, a bar stool; that it might have been because I'd been used to training on a daily basis and had recently fallen out of the routine. What the doctors did say was that if I'd taken the Spanish doctor's advice, or if I'd decided to leave it for a couple of days, or if I'd allowed myself to fall asleep, the damage would have been permanent. As it was I was confined to hospital for several days and the first person to come and see me was Sir Matt Busby. He was very kind. He brought me some fruit and we sat and talked for a while about the old days and what I was up to. As he was leaving the room he turned and said, 'It's about time you were back playing again, isn't it?'

I wasn't sure what I wanted to do. All I knew for certain was that I didn't want to lie around a hospital and that I did want to get back into training. The thrombosis had given me a scare. You make promises to yourself at moments like that and I thought, 'Get back on your feet, go back to Old Trafford and see how it goes.'

Docherty had taken over from Frank O'Farrell by then and Paddy Crerand arranged for me to meet him for a chat. I was

In animated discussion with Tommy Docherty. Things later became more animated. (© Brenard Press)

impressed by him. His great point is that he loves the game. His whole life has been football and he has an ability to communicate his enthusiasm. He wanted to play the game the right way, the way that Manchester United had always played football, the way United should play football – going forward, always on the attack, always looking for goals. We agreed that I should go back. Docherty had been very persuasive. He told me, 'Look, I know you like a night out with the boys, but as long as you train hard and play well, I'll keep any problems you have out of the press. That'll be just between you and me and no one else.'

Obviously, I wasn't one hundred percent fit. I'd been off for some two years and my leg was still hurting a little and I told him that I didn't want to go straight back into the first team until I felt a hundred percent fit. He played me a few weeks later, of course. That was Tommy's way. I should have realised then what he was like. As David Sadler, who was playing for United then, said to me, 'If Tommy Docherty says "Good Morning" to you, go outside and check the weather.'

But I kept at it. The skill factor didn't concern me. The ability never goes. I can still do things today that I could do 20 years ago, and I was only 26 then. The pace wasn't what it had been, of course, but that was only because I hadn't been playing for a while; and I was always able to regain my fitness very quickly. I stopped drinking completely. I really worked hard those last three months. I worked on my sprinting and running backwards and my off-the-mark acceleration. I went back every afternoon for extra training with Paddy Crerand and Bill Foulkes. And while I wasn't back to my peak, it was getting better every week. I started going past players again without them being able to catch me as they had been when I first started on my comeback. I was enjoying the game. I was looking forward to the match every Saturday. Then, when I scored against Tottenham Hotspur, I knew I was really ready.

A couple of weeks later we were playing Plymouth Argyle at Old Trafford in the F.A. Cup and I lay in bed the night before planning what I was going to do. It was like the old days again. I thought to myself: 'You're back to where you used to be, this is the perfect opportunity to show that George Best really is the best.'

It never happened. It was never allowed to happen. Tommy Docherty dropped me from the team.

I missed training on Wednesday morning. It was the first training session I had missed. I made up for it. I went in on the Wednesday afternoon, after the other players had knocked off for the day, and put in my day's work, and then a little bit extra to make up for my morning absence. Tommy Docherty had been quite specific about this. When I came back to Old Trafford he said to me: 'I know you like a night out with the boys. If you have one and you miss a morning's training you'll have to come back and do it in the afternoon. But no one will ever know about it. It will be between you and me. That's the way we'll work it. I promise you.'

I went in as usual on Thursday and again on Friday. Docherty never mentioned anything to me, not a word. I arrived at the ground on Saturday and started taking my jacket off when I was called in to see Tommy Docherty and Paddy Crerand in the referee's changing room. Docherty said: 'I'm not playing you today.' I asked why not. Paddy, who was then assistant manager, said, 'Because you didn't turn up for training on Wednesday morning.'

'But I came in on Wednesday afternoon – that's what we agreed. That's what you promised.'

Docherty said, 'It doesn't matter. You're not playing.' I asked him again, 'Why not?'

He replied, 'I can't let it be seen that you are bigger than me.'

I said, 'If I'm not good enough to play against Plymouth Argyle, then I'm not good enough to play against anybody.'

Paddy said to me, 'Come in for training on Monday morning and we'll forget it.'

No, that's not the way I work. Forget Monday. Forget Manchester United. Most of all forget Tommy Docherty. I ain't coming back. Paddy and Docherty left. I cried.

I walked out of the referee's room and into the players' room where the team gathers for a drink after the match. United won 1-0 but I didn't see the match. I didn't go to the dressing room. I stayed in the players' room. After the match I had a couple of beers with the players, and told them, 'This is it.'

They were as shocked as I was. One or two of them were

actually quite angry about what had happened. I remember Brian Kidd and Sammy McIlroy asking what the hell Docherty was up to. Then, slowly, everyone started drifting away. But I stayed behind. When everyone was gone I walked up into the stands and sat up there by myself.

I was choked. I looked down and remembered the great European games and the championships and the goals and the roar of the crowds. The thoughts and the memories blurred together into one feeling of utter, incredible sadness. I started to cry again. But there was no going back, not this time. It was 1974. Busby had gone. The great players had grown old. Managers were starting to come and go through a revolving door. The atmosphere was not the same any more. I regarded Manchester United as the greatest club in the world. It had always been a family club. Now the wide boys were moving in.

And there was Tommy Docherty. This man had promised me one thing and then gone away and done something else entirely. I couldn't work with someone like that. You can't say, looking at his record, that he was a bad manager, because he did well with United. He won them the F.A. Cup. But off the field he was never really capable of handling the responsibility of managing a great club like United. Great managers have got to be big men both on and off the field. They've got to be able to mix with their players yet at the same time remain aloof from them. Bill Shankley of Liverpool, Bill Nicholson of Spurs and Jock Stein at Celtic were able to do that. They were honest men. Docherty was not. It comes down to one word. Integrity.

Look what happened to Paddy Crerand. He'd been in the referee's room when Docherty told me I was not playing and I told him that, in that case, I would never again play for United. Docherty had just made Paddy assistant manager and promised him that he would be there for ever. Docherty had him out shortly afterwards. Docherty was like that. He would make a promise – then he would break it. I didn't want to work with a man like that. I wasn't going to work with a man like that. People say to me, Tommy Docherty is a lovable rogue, he's a character. He may be a lovable rogue – but character is something he does not have.

I sat in the stands for 20 minutes. Then I got into my car and drove away. For ever.

I regret walking out on Manchester United. I wish I hadn't walked out. I wish I had been able to handle my problems in a different way. I don't for one moment regret walking out on Tommy Docherty. He lied to me.

Chapter Eight

A Game of Numbers

W ALKING OUT ON my job, my life, with a flurry of state-
ments announcing: 'That's it, I'm off. Goodbye,' was
all very well, but it left me facing the awful, empty question:
What do I do now? When, back in 1972, I first informed
Manchester United that I was through with football, it was
not yet the end. But I had started the slow, painful, messy
process of breaking away from the sport that had made me
a star and torn out my emotional guts.

The trouble with football was that it had always been more
than a job to me. It had been a passion for as long as I could
remember. It had also been a routine that had filled my days,
professionally since I was fifteen years old, and before that for
as long as I have a memory. But now there were no morning
training sessions, no Saturday or mid-week matches, no reason to get out of bed in the morning, no reason to go home at
night, no reason not to have another glass of wine or another
bottle of champagne, or another one on top of that if I felt like
it, no reason not to stay up until dawn trying to get some girl
into bed.

I very quickly got bored. I started looking for something
to give me excitement. The booze kicked in. The women
became a mindless, nameless insanity. I also started gambling. A lot of players do. Professional footballers in Britain
have a lot of time on their hands. Training starts at around
9.30 in the morning. It is usually finished by noon. If you
don't have a family to go home to you are inclined to drift
– into the all-day drinking clubs, into the snooker halls, or,
in my day, into the bowling alleys. And, of course, into the
betting shops – which is why a lot of players end up going
literally to the dogs. It starts as something to do and then goes
downhill from there. Look what happened to Stan Bowles.
Look what happened to my old Manchester United colleague
Lou Macari, who was accused of betting against his own side
in the F.A. Cup match against Newcastle United when he

was manager of Swindon and resigned as manager of West Ham United because of it.

That's how it started for me. I had days of time on my hands so, in between having a drink with the boys and a digression with the girls, I began going to the casinos. At first it was only in the evenings. Then it stretched back into the afternoons. By the end I was in most days, from two o'clock in the afternoons when they opened until they closed in the early hours of the following morning.

I know that gambling was not the solution I was looking for, am still looking for, because it never really bothered me whether I won or lost. It was only ever something to do, a way of passing the time. Yet for a couple of years I was in the casinos every day, win, lose or draw, chucking money on to the blackjack and roulette tables like there was no tomorrow. Which there wasn't. Days and nights ran into each other in a blur of chips and counters and dice and cards. If I lost I didn't lie awake at night worrying about it. I went to sleep and then got up and headed on back to the tables.

I was one of the lucky ones. I lost heavily some days but I also won a lot and I had a couple of big wins which fortunately balanced everything out. It was one of those big coups that eventually turned me off gambling. I was playing with Colin Burn, my partner in the Slack Alice nightclub in Manchester. Colin was a big, fearless gambler, even if he was a bit short, which is either the best way to gamble or a sure way of getting your legs broken.

At 20 minutes past two o'clock one morning we were losing £17,000 between the two of us at the dice table. The casino raised the maximum for us from £100 to £200 a roll. By the end of the night we'd won back the £17,000 – and won another £26,000 on top. I should have been elated. I was not. The turn-around had frightened me to death. I went straight out the following morning and bought myself a new E-type Jaguar. For cash. I just walked into the showroom and said: 'I'll have it – and here's the money.' There was no way the casino was going to get that lot back again.

There is a theory that people who gamble subconsciously want to lose, that it is a form of self-punishment. If that really is the gambler's sickness, then that £27,000 provided me with the cure. The extravagance of it was too much for me, and I haven't gambled seriously since.

I do still have the occasional flutter on the horses. And if, on my travels, I end up in a hotel with a casino I may try my luck with a couple of hundred pounds. But that's all – since I gave up big-time betting after that win in 1975 I haven't visited more than half a dozen times, which is hardly the behaviour pattern of a compulsive gambler. And I don't miss it. It did leave me with one amusing memory, however. It comes from the time I was going out with Mary Stavin, one of my collection of Miss Worlds.

We'd been to the cinema, stopped off at a restaurant afterwards and then gone on to a casino where I won a lot of money. When we got back to our room in a hotel in the Bloomsbury area of London, I threw my winnings on the bed while Mary changed into a negligee. I called down to the night porter, a little Irish fellow from Belfast, and ordered a bottle of Dom Perignon champagne.

When he delivered it he saw £15,000 scattered across the bed and Mary prancing around, half naked and the other half falling out of her negligee. I opened the champagne and gave him a £50 tip which was probably his week's wages.

He started to walk out. He stopped. He turned around and said: 'Can I ask you something, Mr Best?'

I said: 'Sure, what do you want to ask?'

He looked at Mary. He looked at the £50 in his hand. He looked at the 15 grand on the bed. He said: 'Tell me, Mr Best – where did it all go wrong?'

If gambling was a diversion, sex and women have been a madness. I have never been faithful to anyone. I find it impossible to be faithful. I'm not trying to prove anything to myself by this and I certainly don't want to prove anything to anybody else. It is pure, selfish excitement spurred on by boredom and by the challenge. When I was at my peak it was pre-AIDS and it became a game of numbers and then the number multiplied and it became impossible to keep count. And when I was running away it became a sport, a way of filling the void.

I've never been able to walk up to a girl and ask her for a date. I've never done that. I just can't. But as the football got worse I started drinking more and the booze gave me Dutch courage. Not that you needed much of that in those days. Basically it was done for you. I was famous and a lot of the girls I ended up in bed with were famous in their own way and there was an element of mutual admiration to it all. Sex went with the E-type Jaguars and the money and the adoration and it was one way of getting your picture in the newspapers. And the '60s and '70s were a time when anything went and nobody bothered about how many or how often. The hippy bells were ringing and the numbers added up. Actresses, waitresses, shop girls, sisters, mother and daughter – at the same time – two in a bed, three in a bed.

Some were famous, like Sir John Mills's daughter, Juliet and the actresses Annette André and Sinead Cusack, and I have happy memories of Lynsey de Paul, photographer-cum-soap-author Pat Booth, Bruce Forsyth's daughter, Debbie, Stephanie Harrison, who is now married to the motor cycle champion Barry Sheen, and a very pretty girl named Georgie Lawton who turned out to be the daughter of Ruth Ellis, the last woman to be hanged in Britain. I even tried to get it together with Brigitte Bardot. I took her telephone number out of the address book of a girlfriend of mine called Jackie Glass who worked in films; but unfortunately I only ever got the maid when I 'phoned and she didn't speak a word of English.

Others were nameless faces on the pillow. I went out to dinner one night with the girl I was with at the time, Miss Great Britain, Carolyn Moore. We were joining some friends at a restaurant and as soon as we sat down I burst out laughing – there were eight girls at the table and I had slept with every one of them.

The more impossible the conquest the better. I had fathers warning me off and irate husbands looking for me and that was like a red rag to a bull. To make it interesting I made it more and more difficult for myself. There was another beauty queen, a Miss United Kingdom called Jenny Lowe who I was seeing when I moved into my Saturn Five space station of a house in Cheshire. She had given me a photograph of herself and three other girls who were Miss this or Miss that. Out of the four I had slept with three. In my warped mind of the time the set was incomplete until I had slept with the fourth. It wasn't an easy mission. She was married and she didn't sleep around, and it took a lot of hard work and patience; but I succeeded in the end.

I didn't always bother to go to such trouble. In my Brown Bull days it was usually a case of seeing what was available and then taking advantage of the situation. As well as being a pub it was also a hotel, and with the Granada television studios around the corner it was always full of young actresses and models. I had carte blanche there. I had my own keys and I came and went as I wanted. It was so easy.

I remember one very beautiful girl who was staying there. She'd been working at Granada and she came in late, ordered something to eat, had a drink and then went up to her room. I followed her up ten minutes later, knocked on her door, went in, and did it. It was a very quick courtship and I thought: this is a nice way of doing things. I can sit around, have a few drinks with the boys, and then pop up and see her when I'm ready. When I tried it the next night, however, she was not having any of it. I found out later that she was seeing Eddie Shah, who founded the *Today* newspaper and was working at Granada at the time, and that she'd decided that that one fall from the grace of fidelity was enough to be getting on with. That wasn't too worrying. There were plenty of others to take her place. It was a revolving bedroom door.

It was the same when I went abroad. I used to go to Majorca every summer and if Manchester was excessive Spain was even more so. It was non-stop, 24 hours a day, especially if you had the Scandinavian connection which, because of my football, I did. There was a crowd of us and we used to take a villa and when you woke up in the morning there might be as many as 20 bodies scattered around. I was the only one who had a safe bedroom. I always locked it so that nobody else could get in. For the others it was a case of first come, first served, which always led to a scramble for beds.

We had an unwritten rule that when we had an orgasm we had to shout 'Geronimo!' at the top of our voices so that the others could clap. It was all good, clean, healthy fun, or so we thought. Nowadays you would need a medical certificate after every night. Considering what we went through it is very surprising we didn't come down with something every week. I was lucky, though, just as I had been with my gambling. Over all the years I've only been infected twice, which is remarkable considering what I've been through. Once was in Spain. The other time, more hurtfully, was in London.

It involved a former *Playboy* bunny whom I met when I was playing for Fulham. She'd been living with a friend of mine and I stayed with them sometimes. He would get up in the morning and go to work and sometimes I would stay on and watch her sitting on the floor combing her hair, or stepping out of the shower, or putting on a see-through top and I kept thinking, 'Shall I chance my arm?' I never did. I never made a move.

A few years later, however, I became involved in Blondes, a club in Mayfair, and one night she walked in. We hardly exchanged ten words before we were out of the door and on our way back to my flat in Chelsea. Unfortunately for both of us, and much more for her – by that time she was married with children – I found out the next day that I was not very well. There was nothing I could do. I didn't have her telephone number, I didn't know where she lived, I had no idea what her married name was.

I went to the doctor and got myself sorted out and I was sitting in Blondes again some weeks later, chatting to Angie Lynn, my girlfriend at the time, when a girl I didn't know came up to me and said, 'So and so says thank you very much for the present.' I said: 'What are you talking about?' She said: 'You know,' and walked off.

Angie was curious and asked, 'What the hell was that all about?' I said that I had no idea but I would find out and went across and asked her again what she was on about. She mentioned the name of her friend, which was not the name of the woman I had been with. But *Playboy* bunnies always took on these strange working names, and it clicked who she was talking about.

By then, of course, Angie was getting well and truly agitated and to get out of the trouble I was getting into with her I told her that: 'First she was talking about this name, now she's talking about that name, and I don't know what she's talking about. Let's get out and go and get something to eat.'

As we were leaving, just to try and throw Angie off the scent, I stopped and said to the girl, 'I don't know who the hell you're talking about – but don't ever make trouble in front of my girlfriend again.'

Ten days later the girl I'd infected came into the club and I went over and told her the truth. I said that I was very sorry about what happened but that I honestly didn't know that there was anything wrong with me until the following day and that I had no way of contacting her. She said that it was all right, that it had not particularly worried her, but that she had to explain everything to her husband.

'What do you mean, you had to explain everything to your husband?' one unhappy G. Best asked. She coolly said: 'Well, I had to tell him what was wrong, didn't I – and who it was.'

She could have been getting her own back, and if she was it worked. For weeks afterwards I was slinking around, expecting a crazed husband to come bursting in to infect me with his fists. He never did, I'm relieved to say. Others were not so reserved. I had a spell in Manchester when half a dozen men were looking for me and I had one close call after another.

There was the situation involving a friend of actor Ian McShane's ex-wife, Ruth. I had been out with Ruth and I had introduced her to Ian, whose father had once played for United. After they'd run off and got married I started seeing Ruth's friend, a very pretty girl who worked in a boutique. Her boyfriend happened to be a jealous lunatic who threatened violence against anyone who even so much as looked at her. He started getting suspicious that something was going on behind his back. He decided that it was another young man, who worked in another boutique nearby, who was doing the chasing. He went round to see him one day and from what I heard, threw him through the window. He didn't have the brains to work out that it was me who was seeing her, not even when he passed me one day driving away from her flat where I had just spent the afternoon with her – and not even when he came back one day when I was actually there, in the bedroom. That really was a close call. It was out of the back window and out through the garden with my clothes under my arm.

These near misses became something of a habit for me. I had an office in St John's Street in Manchester where I often did my entertaining on a big couch. The cleaning ladies were forever finding me curled up on it in the mornings with one or two girls cuddled up with me. One evening a girl who was living with a man I vaguely knew came round and made the mistake of leaving her car parked in full view on the street outside. He drove past, saw the car, put two and two together, came to the right answer, stopped, got out, and started hammering on the window. Then someone started banging on the back door and I thought, 'Hell, he's got a friend with him.'

I told the girl that I was leaving, that I would say to whoever was out the back that she was not there, and that she was to stay where she was until I telephoned to say that the coast was clear. I was fortunate. It was not a man but a woman friend of mine, a very striking Israeli girl who was banging on the back door. She'd seen the white Rolls Royce I was driving at the time in the little private car park round the back and had stopped to see if I was in.

I took her by the arm, told her to leave her car where it was and to get into mine and that I would explain everything later. We then drove around to the front and very slowly passed the man who was still beating furiously on the window. I honked the horn as we went past and waved to him. He, figuring that it was his girlfriend in the Rolls with me, jumped back into his car and raced after us. At the first red traffic lights he jumped out of his car again, came round to the passenger door and pulled it open. He was expecting to see his girlfriend. Instead he came face to face with the Israeli. I said, 'Hello, how are you? We're just off to the Brown Bull for a drink, do you want to join us?'

Looking very sheepish and confused he said he would. As soon as we got to the pub I telephoned the office and told the girl there to get out as quickly as possible and to make up her own story as to why her car was parked in the street. But I added that I thought she had got away with it. And as far as I'm aware she had.

Not everyone was quite so gullible. There was another man in Manchester who had a better idea of what was going on – and he was married to the Israeli girl. He threatened me and I was worried about him because he knew a few fellows who were willing and quite able to help him sort me out. Once, when I was playing blackjack in a casino, he stood right behind me and described in graphic detail what he was going to do to me. I was with a friend who slipped away and called the Brown Bull to get some of the boys down, just in case he decided to carry out his threats then and there. He didn't, but I was living dangerously and I knew it. I was not always the villain, however. It worked both ways and sometimes the boot was firmly on the other foot.

One girl I went out with took the opportunity of leaping into bed with Colin, my partner in Slack Alice, when I had to go back to Ireland one week on business. I didn't get angry with him when I found out but I went crazy at her. I went to her flat and screamed abuse at her through the letter box. She locked the door. I took one big kick at it and the door fell apart. The girlfriend who was with her called the police and I had her hanging out of the third-floor window, threatening to drop her, when they arrived. The policeman was very understanding. He said: 'Come home with us – they ain't worth it.'

But they were. I've always enjoyed women and I've never had the slightest inclination or interest in men (or them in me – I've never been pestered by gays). The football was all but over. I had a lot of time on my hands and these sexual adventures were as good a way as any of filling it.

After a while I took to flying women in from whatever country I found them in: South Africa and Scandinavia, Australia, America. I spent a fortune on flights and hotel bills. And it was never more than a few days before the relationship died in tears and melodrama. I brought a girl in once from the States when I was playing for Fulham, a very beautiful girl and only about 18. Her name was Heidi. Everything was fine until I brought another girl home one night. She was very upset and actually telephoned Angela, my girlfriend at the time who later became my wife, to ask what she should do. Angela said: 'Leave!'

I saw her not too long ago. She's happily married with a couple of children and I said to her, 'You're better off where you are than you would be with me.' She said: 'I think you're right.' She had no reason to be surprised, though. I've always been honest about myself. I've told the women I've gone out with what I'm like because if you tell lies at the beginning you have to tell more lies later to cover up the little lies and that is no way to live. I would rather face the music early on and get it out of the way. I've said to every woman I've had a relationship with: 'This is the way I am and I don't want to change and there will be times when I want to go off on my own.' They always say, 'That's fine, that's the way I want it too.'

It isn't, of course. When three or four months later you prove as good as your word and do disappear for a few days, which is what you agreed you could do, it's a different story. That's when the shouting starts. And when the shouting starts I usually move on. Sometimes very quickly indeed.

In one mad 24 hours in Manchester I went to bed with seven different women. I wasn't playing at all. I had really quit and it just worked out to be one of those crazy days. I woke up with one girl. That lunchtime I went to the Brown Bull and met up with one of the girls from Granada who was on her lunch break and spent an hour with her in her room. When that was done I went round to meet the young niece of some friends as she came out of school. She made the mistake of going out afterwards to do some shopping, leaving me in the flat with her cousin. That made it four. Then it was back to my own place and a late-afternoon session with a girl I saw occasionally. That night I took another girl out. We went to the casino and then back to her home. That made it six. Then I went back to the casino, and on my way home I thought: Why not make it lucky seven? It seemed the right thing to do.

It was half-past four in the morning by then, but I took the chance and drove round to the home of a girl I vaguely knew. She was going out with a man I knew and didn't like. He wasn't there but she was. I had never dated her or slept with her before but she let me in and I slept with her through until lunchtime the following day. Then I left, and have never seen or spoken to her since. She made it seven.

I was young and fit at the time. I was still young and fit when I moved to California, a sexual paradise for any straight lad, not too ugly and with a British accent. I'd touched base there in the early 70s. My friend Malcolm Wagner and I were sitting around in Manchester one day wondering what to do. We decided, just for the fun of it, to take £5,000 out of the bank and shoot off somewhere. We decided on L.A. When we got there we stayed with a mutual pal of ours called Ed Peters, who we knew from our Spanish forays. Ed lived in a mansion in Beverly Hills with a guest house where Elizabeth Taylor stayed when she was going out with Henry Weinberg. I found it strange at first but I fell in with the scene very quickly.

Everyone there was talking about the most beautiful girl they'd ever seen. She was called Linda, and was always in Pips, a nightclub owned by Hugh Hefner. One night we went there. We were sitting in one of the booths when one of the people I was with suddenly said: 'Here she comes – she's just walked in.'

It may seem surprising, but I'm the sort of person who tends to stand in the corner and hope that someone will look at me; if they do, I then try and pluck up the courage to talk to them. Mike O'Hara, who was a crazy Irish-American friend of mine, has no such reservations. He'll try and chat anybody up. He grabbed her by the arm and said, 'Linda, come and say hello to some friends of mine who are over from England.'

He introduced us and almost immediately she said: 'You'll have to excuse me, I've got to go to the bathroom.' Mike shouted after her, 'Come and have a drink with us when you come back.'

I thought, 'That's it, there's no way we'll see her again.'

But I asked Malcolm to move up, just in case, and she did come back. And as she sat down she slipped a note into my pocket. When she left to join the friends she had come to meet I slipped into the toilet to see what the note said. It had her telephone number on it and it read: 'Call me tomorrow at 10.30.' So I did and we spent a couple of weeks sunning it up together and making love in Palm Springs. That was where I discovered all the amazing things you can do in a swimming pool. And after that, it was back to L.A.

After a couple of days at her apartment, with Malcolm playing gooseberry and getting bored, we telephoned the airlines and asked, 'Where's hot?' They said Acapulco, and we headed down there to eat suckling pig under moonlit nights.

The maid woke me up one morning when she came in to stock the fridge with fruit and drink. The sun was streaming in through the window. I could hear the birds and smell the last dew before a hot day. Lying beside me was the very pretty Canadian I'd met the night before. Her blonde hair was spread over the pillow and I leant across and stroked the soft down at the base of her back. That moment was something pretty near perfection.

In the States I was in a bachelor's heaven. I wanted to stay there for ever; and in 1976 I moved to Los Angeles to play for the Aztecs. There was an upsurge of interest in soccer in the United States at the time. Pele was playing for the Cosmos in New York and many of the world's other top players, including Cruyff, Muller and Beckenbauer, were following in his trail, lured by the extravagant wages the American clubs were paying.

I didn't believe that soccer was ever going to overtake baseball or American football as the major spectator sport in North America, but it was a challenge; and the Aztecs' owner, John Chaffetz, offered me a very generous financial deal which I was happy to accept. I was also keen to play again against top-class opposition – and there has never been any better opponent than Pele.

There were other attractions to life in Southern California. The weather is excellent, of course. And I enjoyed an anonymity which I'd not known in Britain since I was a teenager. In L.A. I could walk down a street or eat in a restaurant or drink in a bar without being besieged by autograph hunters or people wanting to fight me. As for the women, I didn't even have to go to the effort of chatting them up. They came to watch us in training. We were young and glamorous and European, and if that was not enough, Rod Stewart often came by to join in the practice sessions. The girls were uninhibited. They wrote their telephone numbers on scraps of paper and thrust them into my hand. And if you didn't telephone they came knocking on your door.

I shared a place down on the beach with Bobby McAlinden, who had once been on Manchester City's books, had joined the Aztecs on my recommendation and would later become my partner in Bestie's, the bar we own in Hermosa Beach. It was open house. We were different, with our accents and our haircuts, and we had all these long-legged, suntanned American girls fed up with the local boys, rushing in and out of the house day and night. We had what the Americans call a ball. I added to the collection of sisters I had had in Marbella and London. And it was here that I slept with a mother and her daughter. They were living in the same

Los Angeles 1976. Playing for the Aztecs and through the pain barrier of my damaged right knee. (© All-Sport Photographic)

apartment block as us and they both got into bed with me one night.

When I think about it now it doesn't disgust me. But nor does the idea turn me on any more. At the time, though, I thought it was great. I was playing games. I was like a kid let loose in the sweetshop and I gorged. My days and nights became a succession of one-offs, one-time encounters. But it couldn't last. For all its thrills this period of my life, my first years in the States, left me with a deep feeling of emptiness.

Chapter Nine

The Wallace Affair

T HE MARJORIE WALLACE saga was an unsavoury chapter in a life filled with unsavoury incidents.

For once it was not a problem of my making. It should never have happened. It should never have been allowed to happen. My relationship with Marjorie Wallace was nothing more than a two-night stand. But it ended with me in court standing humiliatingly accused of theft. And by malicious, suspicious coincidence it all began just seven weeks after I had finally, irreversibly, walked out on Manchester United.

I first met Marjorie Wallace some months earlier at Slack Alice, the night club I part-owned in Manchester. She had just been named Miss World. I was George Best, footballing superstar, and some bright P.R. thought it would be a good publicity stunt to put us together. I was at the bar in Alice's one Sunday night when one of the Miss World organisers telephoned, told me that Wallace was in town and asked if they could bring her into the club.

I said, 'Yes, certainly.' I felt a little sorry for her. Playing Miss World in Manchester on a Sunday night when almost everything was closed is not the most glamorous role. Then they started asking for a fee.

'A fee for what?' I asked.

That's the way we work, they explained, those are the rules: she gets a fee for appearing in places. I said: 'She doesn't get a fee in here. She's welcome to come in if she wants but I don't pay people to come in here. People pay *me* to go to their places. Sorry.'

They called back about 20 minutes later and asked if they could come in anyway. It made sense from the point of view of their publicity to have Miss World photographed with George Best and I didn't mind. I said sure. They came in and I chatted to her. She had a glass of champagne. I was in my vodka and lemonade phase and I had another one. I told her that I went to London quite often and could I give her a ring next time I was down. She said, 'Fine.' I took her telephone number.

I called her a few days later to say hello, and then I called her again and told her I would be staying down in London for the weekend and could I come and see her. She said yes. It was a month after I had walked out on Docherty. When I turned up at her mews flat with my suitcase she asked me which hotel I was staying in – which I took to mean that I wasn't staying with her. I explained that I'd not booked anywhere, that I'd only just arrived, that I'd sort that out later once we had decided what we were going to do.

I never had to. We sorted out what we were going to do. We did it and I spent the night with her at her apartment. It was what you might call a brief courtship. On Saturday we went out and did the usual thing I did when I was in London. I took her to lunch at San Lorenzo in Knightsbridge and introduced her to Mara who owns the restaurant with her husband Lorenzo. We went to the cinema in the afternoon, as I recall, and that night I took her to Tramp discotheque in St. James's and introduced her to the owner, Johnny Gold. What she never got around to telling me was that she'd been to all these places before; with Jimmy Connors and whoever else and, of course, Tom Jones.

Saturday night was again spent at her place. While we were in bed the telephone rang. At that time she was going out with Peter Revson. She didn't know it but he only had a short time left to live; he was killed practising for the South African Grand Prix. I thought at first that it was Revson himself on the telephone. It wasn't; it was someone connected with him, and, listening to the conversation, which I could hardly miss as I was lying right beside Marjorie Wallace, it was probably Revson's mother.

I felt very uncomfortable, and by the time she put the telephone down I was very annoyed. I said, 'How can you lie there and talk like that when you've got someone lying in bed with you? The very least you could have done was take the call in another room.' We started having an argument. She asked me who the hell I thought I was to tell her how to behave. I said I was just putting my point of view.

The next morning it was obvious that our relationship had

run its course. She said, 'I think you'd better leave.' I said, 'I was planning to anyway.'

She got dressed and went out to meet a girlfriend. We'd woken up late and I was taking my time getting up when the doorbell rang. I didn't answer it. I did look out of the window. There was a Rolls Royce parked on the kerb and I was pretty certain that it was the chauffeur who was ringing the bell. I moved away from the window so that whoever was in the Rolls wouldn't see, and a few minutes later I heard the car drive away.

In the middle of the afternoon, just as I was about to leave to go back to Manchester, the telephone rang. I figured that it was Marjorie Wallace checking to see if I was still there. I picked the phone up and said, 'Yes, I'm still here, but I'm going,' and put the phone down.

Looking back it was a silly thing to have done. I had no idea who was on the other end of the line and I hadn't waited to find out. I'd assumed it was Marjorie Wallace. As events turned out it most likely was not. At the time, though, I had no reason to think any more about it. I left, got on the train and went back to Manchester. But on Tuesday night two Manchester policemen came into Slack Alice's. They explained that they'd had a call from Scotland Yard and that two detectives were on their way from London to arrest me and take me back to charge me with theft.

'Of what?'

With theft of property from Marjorie Wallace's flat. I said, 'That's ridiculous.' They said, 'Sorry, George,' and took me off to Bootle Street police station.

When they picked me up the police went round to Mrs Fullaway, my landlady since I first arrived in Manchester 13 misty, innocent years before and where I was again staying, and searched the premises. There was nothing there. Then they took me back to the police station and allowed me to call my lawyer, Geoffrey Miller.

I said, 'Geoffrey, I'm at the police station. They're coming from London to arrest me, for theft or whatever' – I wasn't quite clear at that moment what the charge was. Geoffrey asked me what I wanted to do. I said, 'I want you to phone every newspaper you can get hold of.'

The two policemen who had picked me up at the club were

listening. One of them said, 'We thought you'd want to keep this quiet.'

I carried on talking to Geoffrey. 'Tell the newspapers I've been arrested. I want every newspaper to know because these guys have just got themselves into a lot of trouble.' I explained that I was being taken down to London. Geoffrey said he would get down there first thing in the morning and would see me at the police station.

The policeman asked me, 'What was all that about?'

I said, 'Someone has made a real mess here and they're going to pay for it.' I added: 'This is too bloody ridiculous even to talk about.' It was getting late by then. It was past three o'clock in the morning and I sat around drinking tea for the next three or four hours waiting for the detectives to arrive. When they finally got there they put me in the back of the car, without handcuffs, and drove me back down to London. They didn't say a word to me all the way down.

Once in London I was put into a cell. It was the first time I'd been in a cell and I didn't enjoy the experience. When my solicitor arrived they started questioning me. They said, 'You arrived on such and such a day, you went to dinner, you went to the movies.' The police had got the basic idea right. They'd got the wrong day, however. They said that everything had started on Thursday. It hadn't: on Thursday I was still in Manchester. My lawyer queried what I was saying and asked me if I wanted to tell them that. I said, 'I'll tell them anything they want to know because I've got nothing to hide.' The two detectives went back over everything again and again for two hours: where we'd been, what we'd done. They asked me if that was correct. I said, 'No.'

My solicitor was looking at me and he seemed worried. One of the detectives asked, 'What do you mean,"No"?'

I said, 'You've got the sequence right but you've got the wrong day.'

They insisted, 'No, we've got it right.'

I told them, 'No, I'm telling you, you've got the wrong day.'

My lawyer asked me, 'George, are you sure about this?'

I said, 'Sure I'm sure.' I turned back to the detectives and said, 'It's up to you, you can go ahead with this, but I'm telling you, you've got the wrong days.'

One of them got up, said he would be back in a minute and left the room. He presumably went to telephone Marjorie Wallace because when he came back he said, 'It seems as though we've got the dates mixed up.'

I said, 'Too right you have – and you've got everything else mixed up too.'

They went ahead with it, though, and informed me that I would be charged. I was then released. Bail was set at £6,000 – a huge amount of money in those days. My friend and business partner Malcolm Wagner put up his house as surety. Just before I left the police station the detectives warned me not to make any contact whatsoever with Marjorie Wallace. I went back to Manchester and went straight out and hired a detective to do some checking for me, to see if he could find out what the hell was going on. Then, in defiance of the police warning, I telephoned Marjorie Wallace. I got very, very nasty with her. I was in a terrible state, as I'd just heard that my cousin Gary Reid had been shot in Belfast. He went out to buy a take-away and got caught in some crossfire. He died a couple of days after I got back to Manchester. I was very upset by the news, which had brought home to me the problems in Northern Ireland in a very personal way. I screamed down the 'phone at Marjorie: 'How dare you accuse me of stealing?'

I called her back later when I was feeling a little calmer and asked her, more sensibly this time, what she thought she was playing at. I said: 'You must know who took the things.'

She said: 'No, he wouldn't do that.'

She wasn't so stupid as to put that to the test, however. My detective's report made it quite plain that Wallace was not as pure as the driven snow. His report mentioned a famous singer. It named Tom Jones's manager, Gordon Mills who, it seems, knew her so well that he was able to get her into bed in a hotel near her home. It also made mention of a Detective Chief Inspector who was very much involved with her at the time.

She'd told me that she had no intention of turning up for the court case and she was as good as her word. Her passport, which was one of the things that had been stolen, was mysteriously returned to her and she quickly flew off to America. When the case was dismissed the judge said that I was leaving the court without a stain on my character. I should never have been forced into court in the first place. There was no doubt in my mind that the things had been taken back by the person who had given them to her in the first place, and I was quite prepared to argue that in court, backed up by the evidence collected by my detective.

There was another twist to this tale. A Sunday newspaper had received a package from an unnamed man with a note claiming that it was he, the sender, who had stolen the property. The strange thing was that the contents were not any of the things Wallace had originally reported missing. I wonder if the incompetent detectives checked this out. I did, through my own detective – and I'm also certain who stole that second lot of property. The fact that I was completely exonerated didn't satisfy me, however. I felt deeply annoyed at the way my name had been muddied. But in those days I was front-page news, and people seemed to be prepared to believe anything about the wild boy from Belfast who had just walked out on Manchester United.

Chapter Ten

Marriage

W HEN I FIRST met Angela MacDonald James I had all
the same thoughts as ordinary, healthy, sane people
have. I thought about settling down. I thought about having
children and I decided that I wanted three or four. I thought
it might make a difference, especially when Calum arrived.
I love children and I adore our little boy, and when Angela
and I bought our own home together in San José I thought,
this is what I've been looking for. For a short time it was.

I first met Angela when she was 16 years old. She'd been
modelling swimwear at an exhibition of menswear at Earl's
Court, which I was at because of my involvement with a
company that made fashion clothing. I'd tried to drag her
back to Manchester for dinner but I only got her as far as
the airport. She reminded me of that when we met up again
at Ed Peters' house in Beverly Hills.

Ed liked to party. Every time Bobby McAlinden and I rolled
into town Ed would organise a get together for us. He would
call up a few people and say: 'Hey, I've got a couple of friends
coming in from England, why don't you come by?' Most of the
people he telephoned were women, of course, and he would
end up with around ten men – guys like the actor James Caan
– and 40 girls. It was like a mini Hugh Hefner's.

This time Angela was there. She'd come with a girlfriend.
They didn't stay very long. They did a count of the number of
men compared to the number of girls, did a quick turnaround
and walked out. But I did manage to have a chat to her. I told
her that next day there would only be a few people around,
that we would be lying around the pool and drinking wine
and why didn't she come by.

She did. We talked for a while. Then she went to the bathroom – her fatal mistake. I followed her. The bathroom tiles
were too cold and too hard so we went into a spare bedroom
and lay down on the floor. I won't say it was rape; I don't
think she was too much against it. We came out an hour

later looking haggard and she has the carpet burns on the base of her spine to this day.

That makes her sound easy but she wasn't. She wasn't taken in by Hollywood. And she didn't sleep around the way so many girls in Los Angeles do. That was important to me. That may sound chauvinistic but it was still a welcome change. I'd been having my fun without thinking there was anything wrong with what I was doing. To find someone in that environment, however, who didn't behave the way that everyone else seemed to was like a breath of clean, fresh air.

She was different in other ways, too. She was independent and determined. She came from Southend and it takes a lot of self-confidence to pack and leave home when you're 18 and do your growing up in New York, and then move on to Hollywood and end up working for Cher, who is one of the biggest names in showbusiness. I was impressed by her. I liked being with her and we started seeing a lot of each other. She moved in with me and for a while I even stopped sleeping with other girls; I just didn't want to be with anybody else. And I resented her going out with any-one else.

But it didn't take long for the old habits to click back in again. I started drinking and disappearing for days on end and we started having all sorts of rows and fights. One day she got so annoyed that she stabbed me with a kitchen knife. I had been on the missing list with a waitress for about four days and Angie had found out, as she always did – she had a nose for infidelity. When I eventually came back in through my own front door and told her that I was hungry and wanted something to eat Angela wasn't very pleased. She pretended to get the food out of the refrigerator. Then she picked up a carving knife and made a lunge at me. Luckily I turned around and she caught me in the bottom. I ended up in hospital lying to the nurse who was stitching me up that I'd fallen on a piece of glass on the beach.

We were all right after that but only for a couple of weeks and then I was off again. Eventually, and understandably, Angie's patience snapped and she did some disappearing of her own. She had tried it before but I used to let her car's tyres down. This time she made it and went off to see Cher in Malibu.

I had a vague address and I drove up there and broke into the Colony, that supposedly burglar-proof enclave where a lot of Hollywood stars go to 'commune with nature' in beach shacks which cost a million pounds and are not much bigger than the council house I grew up in on the Cregagh estate. I spent a whole day walking around knocking on doors and crawling through backyards. I wasn't sober and I wouldn't let myself go to sleep in case I missed her coming in; and I was very fortunate not to get myself shot by the security guards or ripped apart by a guard dog. I was in a terrible state when she did eventually turn up at noon the following day to take me home to the beach.

It was around that time that a photograph of Angie and Dean Martin's son, Dino, appeared in one of the American gossip papers. That's what finally decided me to marry her. I think we'd probably have done it anyway but that picture brought it on quicker. I wasn't exactly thinking straight at the time and I resented the thought that she might be seeing someone else. I asked her, she said yes, and off we flew to Las Vegas. The whole affair was to be a disaster from start to finish.

There's something in human nature that makes people want to change their appearances on their wedding day and we arrived at the airport looking ridiculous. We were both the worse for wear from the night before and I was the worst – I was drunk. She had changed her hairstyle completely and I hardly recognised her. I was wearing a horrendous American check jacket which I had just bought for reasons I can't fathom. We were both late for the flight because we were both having second thoughts. We took one look and hated each other. Angie had sold the 'exclusive' to one newspaper, but of course the others had found out about it and we had a Keystone Cops chase all around Vegas for the two hours after we arrived.

The actual ceremony at the Candlelight Wedding Chapel was performed to the accompaniment of taped music by a gay priest wearing a lime-green suit. I did not even have a ring and had to borrow one from my best man, Bobby McAlinden. It was a nightmare; when your new wife starts laughing in the

Angie and I on our wedding day, 24 January, 1978, in Las Vegas. She had a new hairstyle and I had a new jacket. Neither was a success. Nor was the marriage. (© Eddie Sanderson)

middle of the service you should know that it does not bode well for the future. The only fortunate thing was that it was all over in three minutes.

When we came out the first thing I wanted was a drink. We went to Caesar's Palace casino. The waiter, a snarling Italian spiv, spilled champagne all over Angela's best friend and I lost all my money on the gambling tables. When we got back to Los Angeles I went out with the boys and got stinking drunk for several days. Things could only get better after that and for a while they did. But not for long. We were for ever moving locations – from L.A. to Florida, back to England, then up to San José. And the fact that there were days when I would rather go out for a drink than stay at home with my wife hardly helped things along.

When Calum was born I really did think we had a chance, though. I went into hospital to try and dry out and after I came out I tried to do all the ordinary fatherly things. I was there at his birth, dressed up in a white surgeon's coat; and I actually cut the cord. I was in the delivery room, pacing fretfully and worrying myself sick. Angie was effing and blinding at everyone, including me. The baby's head started coming out and the doctor was helping it along. He turned and said to me: 'Do you want to cut it?' I didn't know what to say so I said: 'As long as it doesn't fly around the room.'

He said: 'That doesn't happen in here.' So I took the scissors and cut the umbilical cord.

It was a special, magical moment, especially after all the arguments we had had and all the trouble I had caused her. I loved it. I felt proud and happy and at peace and I burst into tears. I made myself all the usual promises: to be good and caring, to give up the old ways and to work hard and build a better life for my wife and family.

When we got home I tried to keep them. I changed the baby's nappy and read him bedtime stories. I decorated his nursery and painted a Disney mural on the wall. And when he got ill I was on hand to help. We were lucky. Calum was the easiest kid to be with and look after. He slept well and never complained or whinged, even when he was teething. He was the perfect smiling baby, which made his illness so much harder to understand and bear.

He was just starting to walk and talk properly when he

came down with croupe. We knew he was coming down with something because he was wheezing a bit but the doctor we called told us not to worry and not to bother bringing him in until nine o'clock the following morning. I went in to check him just before one o'clock that night and found him standing up in his cot, with tears rolling down his cheeks, trying to cry but unable to get a sound out. I panicked. I got Angela out of bed and told her that we weren't waiting until the morning to see the doctor. I shouted: 'We're going to the hospital now!'

When we got there the nurse on duty took one look at him and said, 'It's a matter of life and death,' which is not the most reassuring thing to say to two very frightened parents, and rushed him off into an oxygen tent. He was in there for several days and when we got him home we had to have a special humidifier in his room to break down the congestion in his lungs. He bounced through it all, but it was a terrible strain on Angie and me.

I did something which I hadn't done very much of since I was a child. I prayed. At moments of crisis like that you tend to go back to doing what you were brought up to do. To see him locked away behind the plastic cover of the oxygen tent, holding out his arms and begging you to pick him up and you not being able to was a heartbreaking experience. I go cold even now just thinking what might have happened if I'd been drunk or asleep or I hadn't gone in to check him. It brought home to me the awful distress that so many parents are forced to endure, and I now do what I can for handicapped and deprived children.

I'm involved in a little charity in Southend for homeless children. I send them clothes and turn out at their summer fête. And when I'm in Australia I take time off from coaching to visit schools for mentally and physically handicapped youngsters. I like working with children. I can help them. They can't harm me.

At one school there was a little girl who had never spoken to anyone. She hid herself away in the corner of the classroom. She wouldn't go outside. But I managed to get her outside and had her laughing and pointing things out in her book to me. The staff were impressed, and I was fulfilled. At another place the children presented me with a book of drawings and paintings they'd done especially for me. I'm not a very sentimental person and I don't hang on to mementoes. There are no trophies or medals or honours decorating my flat. But that book is there, and I treasure it.

Obviously the children don't know who I am; but when I'm with them I know who I am. They're innocent and responsive and you get back as much as you put in; and I still have a photograph of a little boy called Jim who is both mentally and physically handicapped. I can still hear him chanting, 'Bestie, Bestie' – and all because I'd taken the trouble to spend a morning kicking a football around with him.

This isn't something I make any big deal about. When I get involved in things like this I insist that no press are invited along. I don't object to staff or parents taking photographs – why should I? – but I draw the line at having the whole George Best circus running up and down the touchline. Some of the organisers try and argue me round. In Australia I played in a charity match for a boy who had lost his leg. The man in charge invited the local press. When I objected he said: 'It's good publicity for you.' To which I replied: 'I need publicity like I need a hole in the head. And I certainly don't need good publicity. I make my money out of being a bad guy.' What I do I do for the children. And they seem to respond to what I give them, which is all they deserve – affection and attention.

It's the same with my own son. I enjoy being with him and taking him out and having him to stay with me. I take him for bicycle rides along the beach and to the zoo and to Disneyland. We get on well and I make a conscious effort to stay off the booze when we are together and usually I succeed. He's not dumb. He knows when I'm drinking and he will say to me when we go out for supper: 'You can have a beer, Dad, if you want to, but you're only having one.' And that's all I'll have. I've never embarrassed him, at least not as far as I am aware of, and I certainly don't have a problem with him. I have a problem with me.

Angela had a problem with me as well, and, to be quite honest, I don't know how she put up with it for so long. I was always running off for a few days with some girl or other. I was unfaithful everywhere I went, including at the hospital I checked into for my alcoholism – while I was there I had an affair with one of the counsellors. If that wasn't bad enough I was bad-tempered and I was always getting into fights. I got

*Playing happy families with our son Calum, who was born in America.
Here we are returning to England for the first time.
(© David Parker, Camera Press)*

into trouble one night with the police who arrested me on a drink-drive charge and threw me into jail. By then Angela had had enough (again) and when I made the one telephone call the American cops allow you she refused to come and bail me out and I had to spend the night behind bars with a crowd of drug-crazed loonies who were screaming and shouting and effing and blinding at the guards, rattling the prison bars and playing their ghetto blasters at full volume. It was as close to a mad house as you can get and I was in a raging temper by the time I was let out the following morning. I wouldn't have gone home at all that morning if one of the staff from the San José team I was playing for at the time hadn't been there to collect me. As it was I only stopped off long enough to change my clothes before going out again to have a few more beers.

I couldn't even get Christmas together. One year I disappeared with a girl and didn't make it back until after New Year. And instead of a proper Christmas present I gave Angela a rose made out of scrap metal which I bought from a man on the beach. It cost two dollars. She threw it in the bin, and who could blame her? It was one hell of a life for her. Yet still our marriage dragged on because for a long time we both thought that there might just be the possibility of sorting out the mess I'd got myself into. There wasn't, of course. Things just got worse, and the affection we'd once felt for each other became harder and harder to draw to the surface.

I started becoming irritated by her extrovert, pushy manner, and her six-hour lunches with her girlfriends and the way she tried to organise everything. She didn't set out to embarrass me – that kind of behaviour is not in her psychological make-up – but she did just that when she fell into what I call the Tramp discotheque syndrome, which is where you insist on hugging every person you see in a restaurant or a nightclub, waiters included and regardless of how well you know them. Then, when we did finally get divorced in 1986 after eight turbulent, inglorious years, she went completely over the top. But after all she went through with me that's perhaps understandable.

We're still in touch because of Calum and she still takes an interest in what I'm doing and who I'm going out with. And in many ways I regret that we're not together any more. But, in truth, I don't think the marriage ever had a chance to work because I was not that chance. I don't know if anything could make me a good husband; but I do know that the deadly dragon of booze made me a very bad one.

Chapter Eleven

The Demon Drink

B OOZE. MENTION MY name and the word comes staggering into the conversation a moment later. Which, when all things are considered, is understandable enough. I have drunk my way through an ocean of the stuff, drunk myself through days without memory or recall, point or purpose, except to blot everything out in a swirl of alcohol.

Booze, so people who know no better take the unwelcome trouble to inform me, ended my career. It didn't. It was a symptom, not a cause, an escape, not a destination in itself. That said, it certainly didn't help. On the contrary, it simply added another problem to the ones I already had. In time it became the major problem.

Yet it all started innocently enough, without any threat of the troubles to come, in Switzerland, where United took a team to play in an annual youth tournament. We were all young boys aged 16 or 17 and one night we went out looking for some excitement, for some action, which, for kids of our age, meant going out into the Zurich night and into a couple of bars and drinking a few beers. A couple of the players were Manchester boys who had probably been drinking for four of five years. They were drinking pints of lager and looking none the worse for it. But I'd never had a drink before. Nor had John Fitzpatrick, and after three pints we were a pair of lurching, stumbling drunken teenage youths.

Our problem was going to be getting back into our hotel. We knew that Sir Matt and his assistant, Jimmy Murphy, used to sit in the café opposite, counting us back in. We had to walk past them to get into the hotel and, in the state Fitzy and I were in, sitting, never mind walking, was difficult. We took a taxi. My head was swimming, I felt like I was dying. At first the driver refused to take us. Then, when he finally agreed to, he said in broken English, in the time-honoured Swiss way, that he was going to charge us for it – and if anyone was sick in his cab he would charge double. The other lads stuck my head out of the taxi window and screamed at me, whatever happens, don't do it, don't even think about it.

When we got back to the hotel the others held Fitzy and myself up and frog-marched us inside past the boss. They put me to bed and that was the first experience I had of a room moving when I was lying down. Fitzy was in a worse condition than me. We'd forgotten to collect his room key so we stuck him in my bath while someone went downstairs again to get it and carry him off to his own bed. We thought, in our muddled states, that Sir Matt and Murphy hadn't noticed but of course they had. They didn't say anything about it afterwards (after all, we were just a group of high-spirited youngsters doing what youngsters have always done) but they didn't really have to; the experience put me off alcohol for quite a while.

But then I started experimenting, first with lager and lime, then on to wine and champagne and occasionally vodka mixed with lemonade. There was nothing serious in any of that, even when I got a liking for the taste. I may have started to get a reputation as someone who liked a drink but that was more to do with the amount of time I was spending in nightclubs than the amount of drink I was consuming. I used to play up to it a bit. When people threw beer cans during a game, which they did now and then, I would pick them up and pretend to drink out of them, which would make them laugh. The actual amount of drink drunk was rather modest, however, as Sir Matt well knew. He kept a watchful eye on his youngsters and he must have known that it was rare for me ever to get back to my digs at Mrs Fullaway's much after midnight, which meant that I was getting a healthy eight or nine hours' sleep before getting up to go training.

There were occasions, of course, when I crept in later and there were times when I came home drunk, but dear old Mrs Fullaway, who was very fond of me, would never have dreamt of reporting me to Sir Matt. But then she didn't have to. He knew what I was up to. I don't believe he ever had me followed but he always managed to have a detailed account of everything I'd been doing. People were forever telephoning him to say that they'd seen me in this bar or that night club and sometimes in both places at once. I think he disliked those unpaid spies. Sir Matt treated his players like men; if you went out and had a little too much to drink that was fine as long as you came in for training the following morning and did what you were paid to do on Saturday afternoon.

Even when a crowd of us made a base out of the Brown Bull pub near the Granada television studios he didn't make too much of a fuss. The Brown Bull pub was an extraordinary place. It was the time when the north of England was the focal point of everything, from music and the Beatles through to acting, with people like Albert Finney making it in gritty films like 'Saturday Night and Sunday Morning'. The Brown Bull just added to the scene. It never closed. It never had any trouble with the police, probably because they drank there too. Sir Matt called it the Black Cow and it was not a nickname of endearment.

At the same time it gave us all somewhere to go, to drink, to relax. Even Bobby Charlton, who usually went straight home to his wife and family after a match would pop in sometimes for a drink.

My problem was getting out of the place. In 1966 after a game in Portugal against Benfica I was labelled El Beatle and the whole George Best phenomenon went into overdrive. Until then I was just a football player. Suddenly I was one of the biggest pop stars in Europe. I enjoyed it at first. I enjoyed the fame and the attention and I enjoyed being recognised. I enjoyed the money it earned me and I enjoyed the women it attracted. At one stage I was appearing more often in the pop magazines than I was on the football pages of the newspapers and teenage girls would crowd into Old Trafford and scream every time I touched the ball. That disconcerted the other players. Schoolgirl screams are not the sounds you expect to hear at football games.

At that time none of that presented a problem to me. I was young and I was fit. I was playing in a great team and I was enjoying my football. And while Sir Matt may have had his reservations about the life I was leading he was hardly going to make an issue of it. I was playing some of the best football ever seen and we were winning games. He did sometimes ask me if I wasn't burning the candle at both ends but he had no real cause for complaint. If I did have a late night I always came in for training and worked twice as hard to sweat out what I had poured in.

Then gradually and without my being aware of it at first the problems were piling up. I started drinking too much. It didn't show at first – I was at an age when I could still party all night and get up in the morning and do my job. It was a dangerous game to play, however. And when I left Manchester United for the last time, when I walked out on Docherty, I started drinking very seriously.

Being on a football field with 50,000, 60,000 people cheering and jeering your name is a sensation you can never match – or explain. If you want to put it crudely, it's a bit like having an orgasm. When it was over, when I said goodbye to top-class football, I discovered that I had exposed a terrible void in my life. And I tried to fill it with sex and alcohol. The sex was all right. It's like scoring a goal. You have that massive high, that feeling of well being and then you have the low afterwards. But you know that the high will come again – that there is always another shot at goal, another bed and another girl.

Alcohol is different. When I was playing I was drinking but I wasn't going out deliberately to drink myself into oblivion. After I stopped playing I did. It was dreadful. Alcohol is not the same as football or sex. You might get the highs and the lows, but a lot of the time the lows stayed low and the high wouldn't come back for a long time, sometimes for months. Yet I foolishly kept searching for it in another glass, another bottle. And the harder I looked the worse things became. In America I once went 26 days without eating a proper meal. I would occasionally nibble a few peanuts or crisps but I couldn't keep them down. All I wanted was alcohol.

I did the same again recently. This time the bender only lasted five days, which is a step forward, but even five days is too long and I wouldn't ask anyone to share them with me. They are periods of sheer madness. It's as if I am trying to kill myself. I get hot and cold sweats and I get the shakes. I'm afraid to walk down the street in case someone asks me for an autograph. If I fall asleep I wake up five minutes later hallucinating. The worst times were when I was playing for San José in California. I was with my wife Angie then and I don't know how she put up with it. I got so low that I actually started stealing money.

Angie was hiding all our cash in the effort to try and stop

me going out drinking but that didn't help. It's different for me. I'm not like other people with a drink problem. I don't have to beg. I can get up in the morning and walk down the King's Road and stop in every bar and be certain that someone would offer to buy George Best a drink. Drinkers are the biggest conmen in the world and at my worst I was the biggest conman. But I would steal money anyway. I raided Angie's purse. I emptied out the large bottle we put our loose change in. One day, sitting in a bar at the beach, I stole money from the purse of the woman sitting next to me – just to buy a drink.

I didn't know who she was. She was just a girl like any other, a normal working human being. When she got up to go to the toilet she left her bag on the bar stool. There were a few dollars in it. I took them. I was earning $5,400 a week at the time. She would have been lucky to be making a hundred. And I took her money. I went back the next day to give it back to her, but it didn't make me feel any better. I felt ashamed. I felt ashamed that I was reduced to taking other people's money. And for what? So I could buy another drink to add to all the other drinks I had drunk so that I could cut everything out.

I couldn't, of course. The drink doesn't make me feel better. The lows far outlast any highs and the lows bring on the kind of depressions that normal people, people who can go out and have a few drinks then go home and get up in the morning, just can't understand. But still I do it.

Some people say that this kind of alcohol abuse is just wilful irresponsibility – that if you resist the temptation you remove the problem. Others believe that alcoholism is a disease. I'm not absolutely certain but if I had to put my money on one theory I would say that it is a disease. After all, nobody sets out and says: 'Right, that's it, I've got a beautiful home, a couple of cars, a couple of beautiful kids, a good job and I'm going to go out, get drunk, end up in prison, lose the house, the kids, just give it all away.' But I've seen that happen. I've seen ordinary, responsible, happy-go-lucky people crawling on their hands and knees through their own vomit to get to the dustbin to see if there's anything left in the bottle they threw away the day before. I'm not talking about dirty old tramps. I'm talking about businessmen and policemen and lawyers and doctors and professional football players. It has to be a sickness, there can be no other convincing explanation. Because how else do you explain why, when I go out with some friends, they can have a few and go home – and when I go home and get up the next morning all I can think about is going out for another drink?

Partly, I suppose, it could be linked back to the Belfast idea of what a good time is. When they talked about a night out in Belfast they were basically talking about going to the pub or the social club. They did not say they were going out to get drunk, they never put it in those words. But when they went out they would sit there until closing time, drinking as much as they could, before staggering home; and, for many, the drunker they were, the more they thought they'd enjoyed themselves. That idea was programmed into me when I was a child. That's not to say it's an excuse. It's not. It's more a way of life and the Troubles haven't made matters any easier – there are a lot of unhappy people in my home town and alcohol is the easy and, for some, the only escape.

If I got drunk quickly it might have made my problem easier to handle. But I don't. I can drink for day after day and to all intents and purposes I look and act normally. It amuses me when it doesn't annoy me the way people insist that they've seen me staggering out of some pub or other and falling down in the street. I rarely do that. Before the shakes kick in (and it can take five or six days of heavy drinking before that happens) I still appear reasonably sober. Even people who know me well say 'You can't be an alcoholic – you weren't drunk when I saw you.' What they don't know is that I might not even remember seeing them or talking to them. I'm locked away in a world of my own.

Of course, if you drink as much as I do you're going to fall down occasionally. On a flight to Australia I fell down in the passageway in First Class and sent the drinks trolley careering through into Economy. I told the stewardess that I'd tripped – what else are you supposed to say when you've made a fool of yourself? Another occasion when George Best's famous sense of balance deserted him was when I fell off the bicycle I used to ride around on at the beach in Los Angeles. I came home covered in cuts and bruises. Angie didn't believe me when I said I'd fallen off my bicycle. She thought I'd got into another fight. I hadn't. The only fight I was in that night was with the bottle. And that was a fight I never won.

Angie did her best to help me. She would plead with me and lock the doors and take my money. She would put sleeping pills into my coffee. When that didn't work she hit me over the head with a plank. I just turned around and smiled. Then I went out for a drink. I didn't come back for four days. I needed a drink. It was as simple as that. At the same time it was as difficult as that. It was the dreadful period of my life and it was hell for Angela. I tried to rein back but I couldn't. I tried moving. I thought that if we changed locations it would make matters easier. It didn't and sometimes it made everything worse.

When I first arrived in Los Angeles with Bobby MacAlinden we opened a bar called Bestie's on Hermosa Beach and moved into a rented house nearby. Then we bought a flat. Then I set up with Angie in a flat on the beach. Shortly afterwards we moved to Fort Lauderdale in Florida where we had another four 'homes', if you can call them such. It was not until we got to San José that we actually bought a real place of our own. It was a house, a pleasant house with a pool and a view over the valley, and that was the closest we ever got to what you might call 'home life'. But no matter where we were the bottle went with us. I used to sneak out of the house. If Angela had hidden the car keys I would walk, sometimes for up to eight miles, stopping off in bars on the way. And if Angela had taken my money I would go to bars where I knew people would buy me a drink. I was conning my way around California.

Finally, after a year of this, after weeks of block-out binges and days on end when I didn't go home, after countless depressions and hours spent wrestling with the shakes, we decided that something had to be done. We had a meeting. Not a heavy meeting, more a discussion. The General Manager of the San José team was a man called John Carbray and he had been very supportive towards me, even during the worst of times when I obviously was so drunk that I didn't know where I was. He told me that the most important thing, as far as the team was concerned, was for me to get myself sorted out. We decided, by mutual agreement, that I should check into the Hayward Hospital halfway between San José and San Francisco where they run a drugs and alcohol

Myself with Bobby MacAlinden after a training session with Rod Stewart, a good footballer who still has ambitions to make the Scottish squad.

rehabilitation course. Angie agreed. In fact she was delighted – no woman, however much she might love a man or want to be with him, can tolerate indefinitely the kind of life I was giving her. The club's insurance agreed to pay 80 percent of the cost of the treatment and on 2 March, 1981, John drove me to the clinic.

My hospitalisation did not get off to the most auspicious start. My son Calum had been born one month before and Angie was at home nursing the baby. No sooner had I checked in than the police came to see me. They told me that a woman who lived across the road from us in San José had filed a complaint saying that I had broken into their house the night before I went into hospital, and gone into her daughter's bedroom. Angela was devastated. She had just given birth to a child. I was away in hospital. Now she receives a call accusing me of entering a strange girl's bedroom with, we presume, some evil intent.

To this day I don't know exactly what happened. When I got out of prison, which is the way I remember the hospital, I went to see the police as instructed. They said that there were no specific allegations. I was not being charged with statutory rape, just with entering the premises. The girl said that she'd recognised my voice. I asked the police how it was possible for her to recognise my voice as I'd never once spoken to her. She also said that the man who had been in her room was tall and well built. That was hardly a description that fitted me: I'm not tall, and after all the binging I was doing my body was as thin as a rake.

I told the detective in charge of the case: 'There's no way this could have been me. On the night she's talking about I don't remember coming home – I was in a state. I had had a night out with the boys and I certainly wasn't in any condition to force my way into a house without waking up the whole neighbourhood.'

The detective said: 'To tell you the truth we couldn't find anything to link you with any illegal entrance. There was no evidence of a forced entrance and if you were as drunk as you say you were – and from what we gather you were – I can't imagine that you were capable of silently breaking your way in.' He said that unless I heard from them, they wouldn't push the matter any further.

And they didn't. That was the end of it. I never heard anything more about it. It didn't make things any easier for Angela, though. It just added to the problems she was facing, and she wasn't very happy when she came to see me at the Hayward on the first visiting day. She didn't like me being in the hospital, and this made it doubly hard for her. How she managed to get through it all I don't know. I have to admire her courage and determination.

I wasn't finding it very easy, either. I didn't like the hospital and I found it difficult to come to terms with the treatment. The counsellors there took you through the general aspects of your problem. They asked how much you drank, how your health was generally. Then they would make you write out the details of the trouble your addiction was causing. They made you write out ten examples of where you had let yourself down and six examples of how your drinking had caused you trouble with the police, your family, financially.

Another question was, 'What are your six worst defects?' Mine, I said, was conning, the way I used my celebrity to hustle drinks in bars, often from strangers. Then I said that I was guilty of putting things off until tomorrow, because there would always be a tomorrow.

They had a treatment called the love seat, which was anything but. It was a swivel chair in the middle of the room with 30 people gathered around you. Everyone in the room is going through the same treatment as you and it's a real cross-section of people who are in-patients there in the special ward; young teenagers, old-age pensioners, doctors, lawyers, people from all and every walk of life. The counsellor hands out a questionnaire with a list of 30 things that are wrong with the person up there in the 'love seat'. The other patients tick off each defect and they can tick off all 30 if they want.

Then they take it in turn to read out what they've marked and you have to turn round on your swivel chair to face the person making the charges. I thought it would be all right. I thought that I'd got on with everybody, that I was popular, that I was behaving myself, that I was playing the team game. I was wrong. Thirty people said that 'George thinks the treatment is a joke.' Thirty people said, 'George doesn't mix. George thinks he's better than us.' And so it went, on and on, all the way around the room. I started crying. Really crying. I cried my eyes out. It was hurtful and humiliating and I wanted to hide. But I couldn't. I was stuck up there in that 'love seat' listening to people tell me how unlovable I was.

In a way it helped me. I felt better for it. I felt that I had learnt something about myself and by so doing I would be better able to come to terms with my alcoholism. It certainly helped me come to terms with the death of my mother. It also, in a way, helped me come to terms with myself. There's a theory that a lot of famous people retreat into drugs or drink because deep down they don't think that they're really worth the attention which is lavished on them. Angela's mother once said to me that I walk into a room the wrong way. I asked her what she meant. She replied that I should walk into a room as if I owned it, that I had to feel as if I had got where I was because I deserved to be there because of my talent, and I had to show that in my body language. She said that people admire me and that I have to reflect that admiration. She said I didn't, and looking back, maybe that was it, perhaps I felt that I didn't deserve the attention and the admiration.

I thought, 'Maybe she's right,' and tried to change. I started walking into rooms with my chest stuck out. But it only lasted two months. After that it was back to slipping in quietly, to being rather relieved if people didn't recognise me. There was deception in the chest puffing, as there was in my behaviour in the hospital.

Drunks are great liars. They are great conmen. I started going through the motions and giving the counsellors the answers they wanted to hear. After 18 days I was discharged with a clean bill of health. I hadn't deceived everyone, however. There was one man at the hospital who knew what I was up to. He wasn't a full counsellor, more a counsellor's assistant. He was a nice man, with an Irish background, and we used to speak to each other whenever we bumped into each other in the corridor. Just before I left he called me over and said, 'I'm going to tell you, George, you ain't conning me. You might be conning the rest of them – but you ain't conning me.'

He was right. As soon as I left I knew I was going back. The day I came out of hospital I said to myself, 'Right, I'm not going to drink for 12 months.' Which meant, in effect, that I was planning to go back on the drink in 12 months' time. At first, though, things were better. Being 'dry' improved relations with Angie, of course. I started doing what other people would call normal things. For me, 'normal' had been going out and getting drunk. Now I would go shopping with Angie and take her to the movies. We would go out to a restaurant once in a while. The problem with my alleged break-in to the house across the road went away. And I started taking a proper interest in my family.

I put my mind to things. One day Angie started talking about getting someone in to paint a mural on Calum's bedroom wall. I said, 'Don't get anyone in, I'll do it.' I'd never painted before, but I did it. I locked myself in the room for two weeks and painted this spectacular mural filled with all the characters from the Disney cartoons. Angela was delighted. She was also very impressed.

But all the time, without let up, I was thinking about

Four generations of Best. Grandfather Jock, myself, my son Calum and my father Dickie, together in Belfast.

having a drink, which made me edgy and bad tempered. To all outward appearances I was perfectly normal; but inside I was gasping. The hospital calls this the 'dry drunk syndrome'. I tried to find all sorts of things to occupy me. I tried to make walking the dog and pushing the baby around the garden important. I even built a gym in the garage to try and occupy my mind, to give me something to do. But all the things I was doing to fill my time were boring, and part of the trouble with being a professional footballer is that you have a lot of time on your hands. It was the same as it had been at Manchester United, where we would train from ten through until 12.30 and then spend the rest of the day in a snooker hall or the betting shop or drinking club. It wasn't as aimless as that in the United States. Athletes there are expected to get involved in the local community, to give lessons to children, to take part in community programmes. But that still left me with the better part of every afternoon to fill.

Angela, meanwhile, was trying to get on with her own life

and ignore this snarling beast prowling around the house. She was lucky; she'd made friends with a woman who lived a couple of houses away who also had a young baby. Angie's sister Lindy came to stay with us. And once in a while one of her model girlfriends would come over and spend the day nude sunbathing beside the pool. That was great for them but it wasn't too good for me. There they were, lying naked on my veranda, while I was rushing around gasping for a drink.

The inevitable happened. After not quite a year I went back to the old routine. I decided that instead of being a dry drunk I would be a wet one. I would jump into the car and drive off down to a local hostelry where a couple of friends of mine were tending the bar. At first I would only have a couple of beers and then go home again, but then I started staying on for a couple more. Before too long I met a girl who lived over the hill from San José in a little beach community called Captola. I would go missing and stay there for two or three days before crawling back home again with my tail between my legs and ask for forgiveness and promise I wouldn't do it again before driving away to do what I'd just promised I wouldn't.

I was also having problems on the field, the same kind of problems I had experienced at United. The team I was playing for was mediocre and getting worse. The standard of refereeing was soul-destroying in its awfulness. The coaching was second-rate. I knew how the game of football should be played and I still had the ability to play it. It was there, in San José, that I scored what I consider to be the best goal of my career; one that, when I see it now on television, still makes me wonder how I did it. But what I could do the others couldn't. They couldn't even understand what I was trying to do half the time. Then there was the problem with my right leg which was now ballooning up to twice its normal size after almost every match. After a few months of that I started wondering if it was even worth turning out for a game; that perhaps another beer wasn't a better idea, all things considered. That wasn't the way the club saw it. It certainly wasn't the way Angie saw it. So exactly a year after I had checked out of the Hayward I checked myself back in again.

It was frightening being back in there. The first time I was in I had been made to sit in a group. The counsellor had told me to look to the person on my right and the person on my left and had then said: 'In five years' time one out of the three of you is going to be dead, one's got a slight chance of making it, and one of you will be back here within a year.'

I thought he was joking, that this was just the hospital sales pitch. But there I was, back exactly a year later – and the man who had been sitting on my right was dead. It made you take notice and this time I completed the whole thirty days. If you make it through those four weeks and the hospital counsellors believe that you're going to make it, that you have really broken the habit, that you're what they call 'one of the chosen few', you're presented with an award. It is a medallion with the Alcoholics Anonymous logo on it. After those thirty days I was chosen as the one who had a chance of making it. I was suitably grateful and I did go to a couple of AA meetings afterwards.

I wish I hadn't bothered. Can you imagine George Best at a meeting of Alcoholics Anonymous? An alcoholic I may have been. Anonymous I was not.

I would go in and stand up and introduce myself and say: 'Hello, my name is George and I'm an alcoholic.' At the end of each meeting I had people coming up to me and asking me to help coach their son's football team and attend their daughter's school fête and telling me how much they'd enjoyed watching me play.

Obviously AA works for a lot of people but it clearly wasn't working for me. I was still under pressure. I was still having to play George Best. I wasn't getting away from anything. I was still in the same situation I had been in for years – surrounded by a bunch of drunks, except that at AA there wasn't any booze. So I stopped going to AA. Within a few months I was back in the bars again.

My wife got very angry. She called me a drunken bum. But I don't think she truly believed that, not after what she went through. She learned about the problems that alcoholics face. Certainly I didn't want to go out and ruin my life. That wasn't why I'd started drinking. That wasn't why I became a heavy drinker. It had been a social pastime. It developed into a way of passing the time. It became a means of forgetting the problems I was facing. It ended up as the problem – something that no matter how much I wanted to, no matter how hard I tried, I could not shake off. Like cancer. And cancer is a disease.

There is another theory which is that you are predisposed towards alcoholism, that it is in fact genetic. I know that worries Angie, the mother of my son. I don't let it worry me. I don't use any of those explanations as an excuse. Alcohol is simply something I have had to come to terms with as best I can in my own way. But before I came round to that way of thinking I tried one more 'cure'. I had implants sewn into my stomach.

Whichever way you look at it, California is no place to be for a man who is wrestling with his private demons. Life there is one long temptation. The bars are open all day, the drink is cheap, the women are easy and available; and I succumbed.

Not that I was complaining. I had a good time for a lot of the time I was there. I was not subjected to the constant media attention that had sent me halfway round the bend in Manchester, and I could take my wife out without the risk of being insulted by the first yob we bumped into. And while the alcohol never ceased to be a problem, there were periods when I managed to keep it under some kind of control. After my second spell in hospital, however, it was obvious to both Angela and me that the States was not the best place for me. It was not a case of running away. We both recognised that if things were going to go wrong they could do so anywhere – in Ireland or Spain or England. By taking ourselves out of California, however, by taking the naked temptation off my doorstep, we thought we might have a slightly better chance of making a go of it.

I decided (or rather, Angela and I decided) that I would return to Britain and go and stay with her mother in Southend for a while. Angela was to stay behind and settle up the mortgage on the house and sort out the car and the furniture and all the other domestic chores which it was most unlikely, as Angela was well aware, I would ever do anything about. Then, if I had settled myself down and was behaving myself, she was going to follow me over.

I fell off the track of good behaviour the moment the plane touched down at Heathrow. The first thing I did was telephone a friend of Angela's whom I'd seen sunbathing in all her alluring charm around our pool in San José. I told her that I was on my way to Scotland and asked her to have lunch with me. She agreed. We met at the Cavendish hotel in St. James's and ended up having an affair, which Angela naturally found out about.

But I did eventually make it to Southend, to the house I had given Angela's mother some money to help buy as a nest egg for Calum just in case I made a complete hash of everything, and I stayed on there for a couple of months. It was a nice, pleasant suburban life. I ate breakfast in the morning and watched television at night and in between I painted the outside of the house. But all the time I was subconsciously screaming for a drink and it was inevitable that sooner or later I would go off and have one; and I did.

It was then that I decided to have an implant. The operation itself is actually a very simple one. Under a local anaesthetic a doctor makes a slit in the belly, inserts between ten and sixteen pellets in the wall of the stomach, and then stitches up the hole. And the treatment works. It makes drink nauseating and unpleasant. The only problem is that it can kill you, and I had to go to Denmark for the operation because no British doctor would perform it. After one drink your face goes red. After a couple you start suffering palpitations and your nose starts to block up. Carry on after that and the chances are that you will die, which is what was happening to a lot of people in Scandinavia – they were having the implants and then going out and drinking themselves to death.

I never got close to killing myself but I did make a dangerous challenge for myself of testing to find out just how far along with the treatment I was. The pellets took anything from six months to a year to dissolve and as the months went by I would start drinking beers just to see what would happen. And if nothing did I would have another one. It had been the same with the oral pills I'd been prescribed in the United States. They acted in exactly the same way as the implants. I was supposed to take one a day, and when I did I would go and have a drink to see what the reaction was. I did that once when I was having dinner one night in Lake Tahoe with Angela and her sister and the owner of the San José team. As soon as we had sat down at the table I excused myself and crept off to the bar. When I came back my face was glowing and everyone asked me if I was ill. I said, 'No, I just don't feel well all of a sudden.' I didn't tell them that I'd just treated myself to a very large vodka and tonic to see how effective the pills were.

It was the same with the implants. I was just waiting for the pellets to lose their effectiveness so I could go out and get drunk again. I was only kidding myself. This wasn't a cure; it was another exercise in self-deception. But I was willing to try anything because the binges were becoming longer and the downs were getting lower and at least it stopped me drinking for a while. With those pellets in my stomach it was impossible to drink too much, and when the first lot ran out I went back and had another lot sewn in. And when they ceased to work I went back and had another £80 operation, which is all it cost.

That last implant, however, was an awful botch-up. It was not exactly a backstreet surgery where the operation was performed but it was certainly not Harley Street and the incision would not close properly. The cut became infected and the pellets started falling out. The doctor cavalierly said that there was no point stitching it up again because the stitches wouldn't hold, and I ended up plugging the hole with cotton wool and tissue paper. Eventually I found a plastic surgeon in London to close the wound for me, but after that I promised myself, never again.

That was back in 1985. By then I'd started to resent all the so-called professional help I'd been given, and I still do. At the hospital I had suffered the humiliation of the love seat. At Alcoholics Anonymous I had been pestered. The implants were a dangerous experiment that have left me with a deep and permanent scar on my stomach. And still I drink.

I decided that from then on I was going to cope with my alcoholism in my own way, which came to mean that if I want a drink I go out and have one. It isn't a solution that any so-called expert would recommend and it has certainly not eradicated the problem. It works for me, however, in the sense that it has got rid of that dreadful dry drunk syndrome which would make me irritable and tetchy for months. Instead of saying: 'No, I'm not going to have a drink for six months,' and then going away to count the days, I try and treat alcohol in the way other people seem to be able to treat it. In other words, if I want a beer I have one. I don't set myself limits and in an imperfect way that works.

I still go on binges and I still have some really bad times, when all I do is drink and nothing else – work, love, life – matters. But that doesn't happen as frequently as it used to and my spells in between are getting longer. In the past those binges would last for months – and Angie Best and Angie Lynn would probably correct that and say they went on for years. Now, even if I don't have myself exactly hitched and harnessed, I'm certainly more under control. Sometimes I go nuts. But then I come off it again and go down to the gym and beat myself back into shape and get on and do some work. Seeing Calum helps, and one morning when he was staying with me in Los Angeles I heard him pick up the telephone to call his mother to say: 'We went to a restaurant for a hamburger and Dad ordered a beer – and he didn't drink any of it.' It's that kind of encouragement that helps get you through another day.

I would be lying, however, if I said that alcohol is not still a terrible problem, and I don't like lying to anybody and certainly not to myself. But the hopeful sign is that my spells off the booze are getting longer; and that, for me, is an achievement. It's like being a child again. When I was a boy I would practise bouncing a football up and down on my feet. If I did it ten times one day I would try and do it 11 times the next. It's the same with booze. If I stay off it for three weeks I might try for four the next time. But there's no rigid planning to it. I just take each day as it comes, and things seem to be getting better. They could, of course, be better still. The three things that have dominated my life are football, sex and booze. If I had any say in the matter, booze would come a very distant third.

Chapter Twelve

A Sense of Guilt

My MOTHER ANNE died in her council house, my child-hood home, on the Cregagh estate on 12 October, 1978. The coroner ruled that she died of natural causes. Those causes included alcohol, and for years and years afterwards I felt terribly guilty about it. I still do.

I wonder if I had gone home more often, if I hadn't been away from home, if I hadn't been in America, if I had written, if I had telephoned more often, if I had been there, it might not have happened. For I can't help thinking that my mother drank because of me. The bad publicity I had attracted upset her. It hurt her. It hurt my father too, but he's such a strong character that he was able to ride it out. I remember saying to him when the troubles really began, when walk-outs started: 'Don't worry, I can handle it.' Perhaps I could, perhaps I couldn't. My father could. My mother couldn't. She didn't drink when I was a child. But in the last years of her life she was drinking a great deal.

I don't care who sees me drinking, it really doesn't bother me. When I'm sitting in a bar people sometimes come up to me and say, 'So you've still got your problem.'

I say, 'What problem? I like drinking. If I want a drink I'll have a drink.' It's secret drinking that frightens me. I don't want to lock myself away with only a bottle for company. That would scare the life out of me. That's why I rarely have any alcohol in the house.

The only time I drink at home is when I'm coming down off a bad binge. I have to slow down gradually. At those times I keep a few cans of lager in the fridge. I need a little alcohol to help ease me down. If I don't get it I wouldn't be able to go outside my front door. I suffer from bad withdrawal symptoms. I get the shakes. Every day I'm asked for my autograph. I don't want anyone to see me shaking so badly that I can't hold a pen to sign my name, so I have a couple of beers to steady me because I want to go out. I'm not a hermit. I don't want to hide and I've never been ashamed to go out and have a drink.

My mother was the complete opposite. She drank at home because she didn't want people to see her drinking. She would sit at home in the afternoons, working her way through the bottles of cheap wine she bought from the local off-licence. My father found it very hard to come to terms with. He couldn't understand what was happening or why it was happening. He was always capable of handling his drink. He likes to go out and have a few pints with his friends but he never gets drunk as such. My mother did. That brings me back to the question: why can some people go out and have a drink without suffering any serious ill-effects, yet other people, like my mother and myself, couldn't?

The situation in Northern Ireland didn't help. Everything was getting on top of her. And she really disliked people talking about her famous son. My father never minded people coming over to talk about me. He's keen on football and he quite liked talking about the game. My mother hated it. She was very shy and she didn't want to discuss me. She didn't even like my name being mentioned. When people came up to her and said, 'You're George Best's mum, aren't you?' she always wanted to deny it. On one occasion all this talk about what I had been up to made her lose her temper, which was most unusual because I don't remember her ever getting properly angry. She was out with my father at one of the social clubs they used to go to. It was a place they went to regularly and where they knew everybody.

They had had a good time and they were on their way home. On the way out my mother went into the ladies room. A woman came in and started making comments about me. She asked, 'Are you Mrs Best?' She said she was. She said, 'Are you George's mum?' She nodded. The woman started on about me, saying, 'Your son is this, he's that, he's the other.' My mother flipped. She turned around and punched her, and that must have hurt because she had been a very fine athlete in her youth. Then she rushed out of the toilets and grabbed hold of my father and said, 'Oh Dickie, let's get out of here quick.' My father asked what was wrong. But my mother wouldn't tell him. She just said, 'It doesn't matter, let's leave, please.' He only found out later that she had chinned the woman.

141

With my parents. The celebrations were short lived, my mother died shortly after this picture was taken. (© Daily Mirror)

I was not the only problem facing my mother. Her family was growing up and leaving home and she felt lonely and isolated. She was depressed and she was unhappy. Not with my father. Not even with me so much, but with Belfast and the way things were there. She was going through the same thing that thousands of other people in Belfast have gone through and eventually it just got too much for her. One day she just decided to herself, 'That's it.' And it was.

When I checked into the Vesper Hospital in Hayward, California, to be treated for alcoholism, one of the first things the doctors there tried to tackle was the guilt I felt over my mother's death. They said that it was not my fault, that there were other factors. I still can't help but feel, however, that if I had been there I might have been able to do something. I used to get telephone calls from my family, from my aunts and sisters, asking me to come home and talk to my mother, because I was the only one who really knew what she was going through. It is a case of like knowing like.

Jimmy Greaves, who has had drink problems of his own, was very sympathetic to me one time I was appearing on TV-am. The station was doing a tribute to me and Denis Law, Michael Parkinson, Kenny Lynch and Greavsie were in the studio. I arrived with Angela and our son. I had been out and had a real session and I felt terrible. No one except Greavsie realised the state I was in. He took one look at me and asked, 'Are you okay?'

I said, 'Not really.' He said he'd be back in a minute, went off, and came back with a coffee. Only he and I knew there was a large brandy in it. He knew I needed it. He knew I needed a drink to calm me down.

In the same way I offered my mother what help I could. I did go home and I did try to reason with her. But I knew I wasn't getting through. She would sit there and nod – just the way I would sit and nod when Sir Matt Busby tried to talk to me. She could hear what I was saying but it didn't register. And then she died.

She'd been a good mother, she'd loved me and I'd loved her. However I may have upset her, she never once embarrassed me. But my mother's death does pose the worrying question. Is my drink problem genetic? Was I programmed from birth to be an alcoholic? It doesn't worry me so much as it worries Angie.

Chapter Thirteen

Under Arrest

THE POLICE HAVE always treated me well and my relations with them have on the whole been cordial. They have taken my side when some nutter has hit me in the street and I have hit them back and they have gone running off to complain that George Best attacked them. They have been sympathetic on those occasions when I have been rowing with whichever girl I happened to be with at the time – more sympathetic, to be honest, than they sometimes had reason to be. And back in my playing days they were always more interested in looking after me than looking for me. Even the American cops, who have a reputation for being real toughies, were understanding and polite. And that, considering the problems I've got myself into over the years, is a fair and decent record.

There was one time, however, when the sight of a drunken George Best in charge of a car proved an irresistible target. It began with me on a drinking binge. It ended with me in prison.

It was a Friday night and I had gone out to get drunk. I rarely do that; more usually the binges start by unpremeditated mistake. But once in a while I say, 'Right, I'm going to get drunk.' When I do I never take the car with me. This time I did. I drove down the King's Road to a place called Blushes. I parked the car on a meter and promised myself that I wasn't going to touch it again that night.

I went in and drank a lot and then went across the road to a little late disco club and drank some more. I stayed there until about one-thirty before deciding to move on to Tramp. There is no way I should have driven. There is no way I really could have driven and, as I left, the girl on the reception desk asked me if I needed a taxi. I said I didn't; that it was the King's Road, that there were plenty of taxis and that I was certain to get one for myself in a moment. I didn't. It was pouring with rain and when it's raining taxis in London all of a sudden disappear.

I stood outside for five or six minutes, getting wet and irritable. I was also drunk and thought to myself, what the hell, it's only five minutes to Tramp, I'll take the car. I made it to Buckingham Palace when the police pulled me over. They breathalysed me, put me in the police car and drove me to the station. At around six o'clock on Saturday morning I took a taxi home to Chelsea, got into bed – I was feeling shattered and I was still drunk – and fell asleep.

It was some time in the early afternoon before I woke up. I took a shower and then walked down the King's Road to the place where I'd been the night before, for a pick-me-up. When I walked in everybody stopped talking and started looking at me. Someone asked me what I was doing there. I said I wanted a beer. That's when they told me that they'd heard on the radio that there was a warrant out for my arrest.

'A warrant? What are you talking about?' I asked.

'You were supposed to be in court at nine o'clock this morning,' someone answered.

I didn't know that courts are held on Saturday morning; I thought I was due to appear on Monday. And even if I had known I'm not certain I would have been fit enough to have got there. If you get home at six o'clock in the morning, still drunk and feeling remarkably unwell, the odds are against your getting up and out again by nine. It would have been much better – for the police as well as for me – if I'd been kept in the cell until I was due to appear before the magistrate. But that hadn't happened. And there I was, sitting in a bar drinking a beer with a warrant issued against me. Not that the police seemed to be taking the matter very seriously at that point. As I'd walked down the King's Road I'd passed three policemen who had done nothing more than wish me a pleasant afternoon.

Whether I would be able to walk back down the King's Road was another matter so I telephoned my agent, Bill McMurdo, in Scotland and told him to get hold of a lawyer. He said that he'd arrange that for me, that he'd get everything straightened out, that I was to turn up at the magistrates court on Monday morning, and that in the meantime I was to stay out of the way. I didn't, of course. I stayed out drinking all day. I turned up in first this club and then that one and I didn't make it home until around seven o'clock on Sunday morning. When I got there I found the flat ringed by newspaper reporters. They told me that the police had been there looking for me.

In the normal course of events it wouldn't have bothered me being picked up by the police. But I was right in the middle of a binge. I desperately needed a drink. I know how my system works; I have to come out of these drinking sessions gradually and if I had been locked up for 24 hours I would have been climbing up the wall. So instead of handing myself over to the police I decided to lock myself away inside my apartment for the rest of the day. Just as I got inside there was a banging at the door. I picked up the telephone intercom and shouted, 'Piss off'. I thought it was one of the press men. It wasn't. It was a police inspector. He told me to come out. I hung up and went and looked out of the window.

There were three police cars on the street outside, a couple of police motorcyclists, and two officers on foot. That added up to a lot of police manpower for someone who hadn't murdered anyone, hadn't had an accident, hadn't hit anyone but who did happen to be named George Best. I went to the back window and heard one of the policemen shout, 'He's trying to get out the back.' There was a great rush of policemen crawling over cars and walls. I thought, what the hell, I'll just stay here and ride it out until Monday morning.

I tried to go to sleep but couldn't. I tried to read but couldn't concentrate. I wanted a drink but I never keep any alcohol in the house, which is one way of cutting down on consumption. After an hour I looked out of the window again and everyone had disappeared. I thought that perhaps they had decided to leave it until Monday after all, so I went and had a shower, changed my clothes, had a few coffees, tried to get myself together, but that wasn't working. I was gasping for a drink and it was becoming painfully clear that I was never going to make it through to Monday without one.

So I decided to make a dash for it. I telephoned a girl called Diane who lived directly across the road from me, figuring I could spend the rest of the day with her. But she wasn't too happy about that. She'd seen the police outside my flat and the newspapermen and she kept asking me what was going on. I told her: 'Don't ask any questions, just leave your front door open and I'll be over in five minutes and explain everything.' I looked out of the window. There was no one there. I gingerly opened my front door, braced myself, then sprinted the 20 flying yards across the road to her place. And as I started running six policemen who had been hiding somewhere behind the parked cars started running after me. I made it to Diane's door and slammed it just as the policemen crashed into it. I ran through into Diane's flat shouting, 'Where's the back window?'

She said, 'I don't have a back window.' Which was the way my luck was running that day – there are six policemen from the Special Patrol Group beating on the front door. A van with eight more policemen had just drawn up outside. And I was in the only flat in Chelsea without a back window. It was obviously the end of this Keystone Cop-style chase and I said to Diane that after all that had happened, I was going to have to go out through the front door again otherwise things were only going to get worse; but I thanked her for trying to help.

When I went out eight policemen grabbed hold of me and started bundling me into the van. I said, 'All right, it's a fair cop,' or something equally asinine. That was fine. Except for one of the policemen. He started on about the Irish. 'You get in there,' he ordered, and pushed me. 'You fucking Irish, you're all the same. And you, you little shit, you think you're this, you think you're that.' He kept on and on so I tried to hit him with my head. That wasn't a very sensible thing to do when I was handcuffed and locked in the back of a van with eight policemen.

The man who'd been shouting off about the Irish pinned me up against the van's window and stuck his elbow in my throat. Then the eight of them each had a whack at me. It was the usual stuff, the kind you see in the movies, with the cops shouting, 'Don't touch his face, not his face, anything but his face.' And they didn't; they kept hitting me in the stomach and on the chest with their knees, fists and elbows all through the drive to the station. When we got there I was told that I had to have my fingerprints taken – and that the man who had started the rumpus was going to take them.

I refused. I told the sergeant in charge that I wasn't going to go into any room alone with him. I told the sergeant that that was the officer who had provoked my beating and that, instead of going to have my fingerprints taken, I was going to stay where I was and file a complaint. I told the sergeant in charge that I also wanted a doctor. They had gone a little over the top in the van and my chest was noticeably bruised from the beating I had taken. I got the doctor. I never got to file the complaint. The sergeant I was going to make the report to pointed out that I would simply be wasting my time because there would be eight police witnesses against me and those odds would be slightly overwhelming in any court case. 'It's not as if you don't have problems enough, Mr Best,' the sergeant added, politely, in his best Dixon of Dock Green manner.

And problems I did have, more than the sergeant realised. I hadn't started shaking; I still had some alcohol in me. But I knew that if I didn't get a drink soon I would be going cold turkey. When I come down off a bender I have to come down slowly and I kept thinking, how am I going to get out of this, how do I get to a bar for a drink?

Thirty-six hours after they should have done so, they decided they were going to lock me up until it was time for me to appear in court; and in my state the prospect of that was horrifying. So I did what any drunk would have done – I fell off the chair. For a while they left me there. I could hear one of them saying, 'He's taking the mickey, leave him there.'

After I had lain there for a while they started having second thoughts. They weren't sure whether I was play-acting or whether there really was something wrong with me. It's one thing to beat up George Best in the back of a paddy wagon. It's another thing altogether to have George Best die while in police custody. Eventually they picked me up and held me in a chair and one of the police officers started digging his thumb nails into the backs of my fingernails. The idea of that is to provoke a reaction, to see whether you are faking or not. It hurt, it really hurt. The pain was excruciating, and one of them said, 'He must either be very brave or there really is something wrong with him.'

Just to make sure, one of the policemen dug his thumbnail in again. I wanted to scream but I didn't. When I was young the one thing I couldn't stand was having my feet tickled. So naturally enough, that's what my sisters used to do to me when they decided I was to be punished for some little misdemeanour or other. They used to pin me down on the floor and tickle them and tickle them until I thought I would go crazy. Finally it got to the stage when I decided that I had had enough of this. When I was 15 I went away to Manchester. When I came back my sisters tried it again. This time however, I refused to let them get the better of me. They held me down, as usual. But instead of shouting and kicking as I used to do, I just lay there and concentrated, concentrated on anything other than what they were doing to me, and it worked. Now it doesn't bother me if people touch my feet.

That was what I did in the police station. I ignored the pain in my hands and focused my thoughts on getting out of there. Eventually they called an ambulance and I was driven to hospital where I was put in a bed. Two policemen were stationed outside my room. A doctor came in and saw the bruising on my chest from the beating and on my wrists from where the handcuffs had dug in. He asked me what was wrong and I said that I wasn't going to go back to the police station because I was in pain and I wasn't feeling very well and any other excuse I could come up with and he said, 'Okay, I'll be back in a minute to have a look at you,' and left the room.

The moment he went out I jumped up and dashed for the window. I believe that everyone shapes their own destiny, that each individual has the freedom of choice to make of his life what he will. There are occasions, however, when some greater guiding hand appears to manifest itself and this was one of them. No window. No window in the flat. No window in the hospital room. No bleeding windows anywhere.

The doctor came back, examined me and ruled that I was well enough to be returned to jail. I decided to make a run for it on the way out. The two policemen, however, clearly knew what I was up to, for the moment we got out onto the street and I thought, 'This is it, I'm off,' they grabbed hold of me. One grabbed hold of my arm. The other grabbed hold of my shirt sleeve which ripped. I tried to get the shirt off but that wasn't getting me anywhere; they'd got a vice grip on me by then. 'Not as fast as we used to be, are we Mr Best?' one said.

'Doesn't seem like it,' I replied as they hustled me into a van, and drove me back to the station, holding me all the way to make sure there were no more antics.

There weren't any. Twenty policemen, with no regard for their personal safety and even less regard for mine, had heroically brought one drunk driver to book, and my weekend on the run was over.

Chapter Fourteen

Trial and Prison

I WAS SHAKING when they brought me before the magistrate on Monday morning. The alcohol was wearing off, the hangover was setting in. It's not a situation I've ever been able to deal with well. I feel ill. I can't think clearly. I find it difficult to talk. I want a drink, not a lot but enough to cushion the re-entry. Most of all I want to be left alone.

Angie Lynn was there with Bill McMurdo and my solicitor. I was given the choice of accepting the sentence of the magistrate or going for trial before a jury. I accepted the magistrate. The charges were read out. Drink driving. Failing to appear in court on Saturday. Assaulting a police officer.

The magistrate said, right, three months, and I was led away. I knew from the mood of the court and the tone of the magistrate that I was likely to go to prison. I hadn't expected to be sent down for three months, not for what I had done which, when you come right down to it, was drinking and driving, having myself thumped by eight policemen and failing to appear in court on a day when I didn't know the courts sat.

I was given leave to appeal. An appeal usually takes three to four months. I was back in court three weeks later, stone cold sober and neatly dressed, with the demons back in their cages. It was the week before Christmas. Three months, the judge confirmed, and I was on my way to Pentonville. Wonderful timing, Christmas, New Year, my son's birthday.

It wasn't as bad as I'd imagined, not on that first night at least. When I'm at home I often find it difficult to fall asleep; my mind races and the thoughts pile in and I toss and turn. But not in jail. The night they arrested me and locked me up in the cell, and despite all the rigmarole and the bally-hoo and the ducking and diving, I'd climbed into my bunk and slept with the innocence of a child until they woke me in the morning. It was the same at Pentonville. I read an article in a newspaper a few days later, purportedly written by a man who was in the cell next to mine, and he said that he had heard me crying all night. The reality was exactly the opposite. In prison those concerns that kept me awake at home seemed to evaporate and I slept soundly.

On the following morning, however, the misery of prison life struck me. I thought I was in for a bad time when I arrived because the warden who checked me in had a Manchester City tea mug placed ostentatiously on his desk. But all he said was, 'It's a shame to see you in here.' He was quite decent about it. He was just about the only decent thing in there. Prison life is appalling. Being locked up didn't bother me unduly; but the degradation certainly did.

You share a cell. When you get up in the morning you have to share one toilet with 60 other men. You are made to 'slop' out your cell's night bowl of accumulated excrement and urine. The stench is stomach-turning. The food is inedible. And it's all done with malicious intent. They're not taking away your freedom. They're taking away your dignity, and the eight days I spent in Pentonville were an unreconstituted nightmare.

But I was lucky, because after I had been inside for a week I was transferred to Ford open prison. There are a lot of windows in Ford and every one of them is open. These were not the windows I was going to climb through. When you first arrive there the governor or the assistant governor holds a little meeting and tells you, 'The gates are open, so if you want to go, go now. But remember, if you do, you're going straight back to Pentonville.' And I certainly wasn't going to climb through a window to make my way back there.

An open prison is not the holiday camp some people might think it to be, but it's still a world away from the squalor and humiliation of an establishment like Pentonville. You sleep in a long narrow wooden nissan hut with six or seven guys on each side. The doors are not locked. There's a cinema. And while there's an imposed regime – you have to get up early for parade and roll call and keep your bed area tidy – you're allowed a fair bit of time to yourself. My job was making tea and coffee for the officers and keeping the officers' area clean. The rest of the time I spent in the gym, training like a lunatic, and I came out far, far fitter than when I went in.

There was talk of my playing in the prison football team,

and Malcolm Holman, the officer who coached the side, said, 'I don't care if he's George Best or Pele – unless he's willing to do hard work training he won't get a look in.'

There was never any question of that. I wasn't interested. I wouldn't have minded a kick about with the other inmates if it had been inside the prison. But the only game they were scheduled to play was outside the prison compound, and that would have been a shambles. There were press men camped outside, long lenses at the ready, waiting to snatch a picture of me having my legs hacked out from under me by a bunch of so-called hardened criminals. I had no intention of playing clown in that circus. The assistant governor agreed with me. He didn't go so far as to say that I couldn't play. But he did suggest that it would not be a good idea if I did, so I didn't. I never even saw the team play. Nor did I get involved in the coaching side. I love coaching, but these were hardly the most convivial circumstances in which to exercise that talent.

No one minded. I never got any hassle while I was in there. Even the officer everyone was frightened of turned out to be a decent enough man. We called him Drunken Duncan, and one of the first things I was told when I got there was to stay out of his way. He never hit anybody. He never got physical. But he made it a point of honour to bark his commands. He was the only one who called me Best, everyone else called me George. It was Best this, Best that. And make it snappy, Best.

The worst part of Ford, the worst part of any prison, is not being able to communicate with the people outside you care about. At the time I was very involved with Angie Lynn. I thought I was passionately in love with her. And if I wasn't I was certainly infatuated, and not being able to talk to her was a new and emotionally frustrating experience. I haven't always been the greatest communicator, either with the people who employed me or the people who at various times have cared about me. I find it difficult to express my feelings. Not wanting to or being bothered to, and not being allowed to are very different things, however, and like most of the other men in there I became increasingly desperate to speak to Angie, to anyone on the outside.

Telephone calls were the greatest privilege you were afforded and people got up to all sorts of tricks to make one.

When I arrived there Victor Melik was there. He was a leather manufacturer from Algeria who had become part of the Chelsea set and I had seen him around the clubs for years. He had been sentenced for fraud and by the time I got there his good behaviour had got him a job in the probationary area where all the telephones were. I decided that Victor and I had more in common than I ever realised and he started getting quite a few visits from me. In that way I was able to make a few more calls than I was officially entitled to.

I was in there one day when Drunken Duncan came in. There was a list on the wall in the probationary area detailing how each officer liked his coffee and tea. Some had it strong with milk, some had it black, others had it with sugar, others without. Except Duncan. Some days he would have half a cup of coffee. Other days he would have a full one. If he had half a cup we figured he was topping it up with the hip flask we knew he carried with him, which is why we called him Drunken.

'Best,' he shouted, 'you come with me.'

I thought I must have done something wrong, though what I could not imagine.

'This way,' he barked, and marched me off to another section where there were five or six cells where they hold prisoners overnight before transferring them to other prisons. Another prison was exactly where I didn't want to go.

'What are we doing here?' I asked.

'We're going to check the cells, that's what we're going to do, Best,' he answered. 'We're going to make sure they're all neat and tidy, aren't we Best, and we're going to take out all the stuff that isn't needed.'

But that was not the reason Duncan had marched me across there. The holding cells are the only place apart from the probationary area that has a direct telephone line and as soon as we'd looked into a couple of the cubicles he said, 'Right, go on then, you've got a couple of minutes, make a call – and keep your mouth shut about it afterwards.'

I started telephoning frantically but I couldn't find anybody. I tried Angie but there was no reply. I tried my agent Bill McMurdo. All I got was his answer phone. I tried a couple of friends but no one answered. I called my sister at home, to tell her not to worry, to tell our father that everything was all right, in fact just to hear a friendly voice. But I couldn't speak to the one person I really wanted to speak to which was Angie. It was pathetic, but prison life has a tendency to draw the pathos out of you.

Then I tried Angie again and I got hold of her. We only spoke for a moment and Angie couldn't understand what the rush was – when she first came down to see me she had checked into a nearby hotel, called the prison and asked to be put through to me as if I too was staying in a hotel. By then Duncan, who was not working to Angie's time-scale, was starting to fret. He was pacing up and down the room, growling that I was not to tell anybody else about this, or he would do this to me or that as sure as his name was Duncan – which incidentally it wasn't – and if I ever got out there was a little pub down the road where he drank and if I ever happened to be down that way I was to pop in and say hello.

That was what it was like inside: long hours of tedium punctuated by moments of elation like the occasional telephone call, a few acts of simple decency, and the occasional late-night feast of chips fried up on a little stove by a couple of the inmates who worked in the gym and had managed to save a few scraggy potatoes from the kitchens.

I was released after two months – sober, in splendid physical shape from all the work in the gym and with Angie Lynn waiting to greet me. I should have been delighted. I wasn't. I don't know whether it was a reaction to prison but whatever it was I just wasn't in the right frame of mind.

McMurdo had arranged to sell the story of my time in nick to a newspaper and as part of the deal Angie and I were to be flown out to the Seychelles for two weeks. I was smuggled out of a side gate and away from the waiting reporters to a nearby hotel where we spent a few days and then we flew off to the Indian Ocean for what we thought was going to be a fortnight of wonderful sunshine. It wasn't. It pissed down for two weeks. I got pissed off. Then I got pissed.

I was in a terrible mood. I was determined to keep my fitness up and I ran every day; and after two months of enforced abstinence I didn't want a drink and I didn't have one. Then, after ten days, I went off to a bar and had a couple of beers. I didn't get drunk but I didn't have to –

if a thousand drinks are not enough then one is too many for an alcoholic. I had started again. I knew I was going to end up on another bender when I got back to England and I did. George Best was back in town and Angie was back in the firing line.

Chapter Fifteen

Best Bites Back

THERE IS A booming growth industry called 'My Life of Hell with George Best'.

Even my ex-wife Angie has been caught up in the act. The headlines are always the same. 'He Let my Son Down.' She even had the gall to have a go at me on her own wedding day in 1989 when she got married, for the second time, to some Californian beach boy. She took the time out from her nuptial celebrations to announce that I'd not shown up as I was supposed to, and that I'd upset our son Calum. But why would she want me at her wedding anyway? And why should I want to be there? I didn't want to be there. I was only doing Angela a favour when I agreed to put in a guest appearance. And, as I see it, it was hardly my fault that I never made it.

It so happened that I was in San José playing in an exhibition game on the day she was getting married. She asked me to come by to say hello to Calum. I explained that I was flying down to Los Angeles to pick up the flight home to London and that I would only have a turn-around time of two and a half hours but that if she laid on a car to pick me up at Los Angeles airport I could make it up to Malibu where the wedding was and spend an hour with Calum. I explained that I didn't want to stand around queueing for a taxi, not with that tight schedule, and that I had to catch the London flight because I had business back in England the following day. She agreed to send a car and I agreed to pay for it. It was not a difficult arrangement for Angie to come up with – she is, after all, the woman who makes all Cher's bookings and appointments and travel arrangements.

I came out of the airport, on time and to the right place. But there was no car. And no car turned up. I didn't have her telephone number with me. Nor did I have the address in Malibu where I was expected. I waited for a little while. Then I telephoned Bobby McAlinden, my partner in Bestie's, the bar we own together behind the sea front at Hermosa

Beach, and went round there for a bite to eat and a couple of beers.

I caught the London flight and arrived back in Britain, sober and fit. I didn't even have a drink on the flight. But that is not the way Angie told it. According to her account I had hit the booze and done another George Best vanishing trick; that instead of going to the wedding I had gone into some bar or other and got myself blind drunk.

It's very disheartening to read stuff like that about yourself when it hasn't happened – but then 'George Best gets drunk and misses wedding and upsets his son' obviously makes a better story than 'Best left stranded at airport', especially if there's an accompanying photograph of Calum supposedly looking miserable because his father hasn't turned up.

I asked Calum about it the next time I saw him, which was when I went over to be with him the week before he started a new school. I asked, 'Were you upset because I didn't get there?' He said, no, he was looking fed-up because the wedding was boring. I find it very sad that I should have to ask my own son for the real truth about something that should never have been made into a story in the first place.

But for others the temptation to make money out of me is irresistible.

A couple of weeks with me and then it is straight to the typewriter to pound out another chapter in this technicolour tale of misery and betrayal. I seem to be an endless source of income to every woman with an eye for the main chance.

When it comes to making capital out of my name no one rivals Mary Stavin. Every couple of years she does a rerun of her own version of 'My Life of Hell with George Best' and pours out the same, lurid accounts of our time together. Mary Stavin is a former Miss World who wanted to be a famous actress and failed. We were together for a couple of years and, to be quite honest, I went out with her to help myself back into, if not the limelight, then certainly into the public consciousness.

It was 1981 and I'd been in the United States for the past seven years, apart from brief visits back to play for Fulham and Hibernian in Scotland. I wanted to be based in London again and I wanted people to know I was back and available; and one way to do that was to go out with Miss World. It suited her purposes, too. I asked her one day what she wanted to do in life. She said, 'I want to be famous.'

I asked her, 'Don't you have any other ambitions?'

She said, 'No, I just want to be famous. I want to be a film star.' Being with me gave her a taste of the fame she craved. But when she said that was all she wanted out of life I thought to myself, 'This is definitely not the woman for me.' But if the relationship was flawed right from the beginning she still got the best out of me. She's the woman I got closest to being faithful to. In all the time we were together I only went with one other woman, which for me is a record.

I first met her at Belfast airport. We were introduced by an old friend of mine, the actor George Sewell who was appearing with her in a play. A short while later I was in Birmingham doing some promotional work for Holiday Inn and by pure coincidence the play had moved there and it was the last night. I telephoned George at the theatre. He knew why I was calling and he said, 'Come down, Mary will be here.'

I met her in the dressing room and while George discreetly went for a walk I asked her if she'd like to come back to the hotel for a cup of coffee before she got the late train home to London. She asked me to stay for the show but I didn't really fancy watching the play so I left her a note saying that I didn't want to be a stage door Johnny but if she still fancied that cup of coffee I would be in my room, which happened to be the room she had just checked out of. Sure enough, she turned up and we sat up the whole night talking. She missed the 11 o'clock train and the midnight train and it was not until nine o'clock the next morning that we made it to the station. I decided to travel down with her which was when she told me that she was living with Don Shanks, an ex-footballer who once played for Queens Park Rangers. I said I hoped he wouldn't be waiting at the station to meet her and she said they weren't getting on and that she was thinking of moving out.

In fact nothing had happened in the hotel room. We'd sat on the bed. We hadn't got in it. We'd ordered some sandwiches and a bottle of wine and when it came I went to grab her and kiss her and ended up toppling off the edge of the bed and falling flat on my face on the floor – which was very romantic and must have impressed her no end. After that we just talked.

I must have said the right things because a couple of days later she contacted me and told me she was leaving Shanks and asked me to come round and help her move her stuff out of the flat. I said I would if Shanks was not there and she said that he'd gone dog racing, so round I went and moved her out of London and down to Windsor to stay with a girlfriend called Madeleine Curtis and her husband Geoffrey. And I moved in with her – with a girl I hardly knew and whom I'd never slept with.

We stayed there a while and it was all very pleasant. Mary got on well with Madeleine, who was Swedish. We used to have Sunday lunch around the swimming pool where Peter Holmes, who went on to marry Joan Collins, would play his guitar and sing the only song he knew (which he'd written himself). It was awful. After seven months of that we moved into a flat in the Barbican and that was worse than Holmes' singing. It was like living in Colditz. If I came home the worse for wear it was an achievement to find my own front door in that concrete wasteland and in all the months we were there I never even saw a neighbour, never mind spoke to one. But we survived that and I survived the attack on me in a pub where a lunatic crashed a beer mug onto my head, and then we moved into a very nice basement flat at the end of the King's Road in Chelsea.

It was then that things started to go wrong. Angela, my wife, had come back from America and I was seeing a lot more of Calum. Angela who got on well with Angie Lynn, didn't like Mary, partly because she wasn't receptive to our son. She never once picked him up or held his hand and that put me off her too. Also the talking had stopped. She wasn't interested in books or the theatre. All she wanted to be was famous. When she went off on a job assignment I took a girl back to the flat. It was the only time I'd ever done that in all the time we'd been together, but, by sod's law, she found out and accused me of using our flat as a knocking shop every time she went away.

The relationship was running out of momentum. It had fulfilled its purpose for both of us – I had given the newspapers the story they were looking for and so let everyone know I was back in Britain and available for work, and Mary had got her photograph taken lots of times, which is what she desperately wanted. She announced that she was going to

America to try her luck in the movies. I said, 'Go ahead, but you've got a problem. First of all you have an accent and Hollywood does not like accents. And secondly, you have to remember that even if you are a beautiful woman there's no shortage of beautiful women in Los Angeles – and a lot of them can act, which you can't.'

When she moved away I went over to see her a few times but by then it was all over, and the last time I saw her she told me that she wasn't coming back, that she was going to be a movie star and that she'd met a man at the acting school she was attending whom she was going to move in with.

Then all the nasty articles about me started appearing. She said that she'd left me because of my womanising. I couldn't understand that as I've never behaved better with a woman. She said I was boozing. That was an exaggeration. I was getting a lot of work. I commentated on the 1982 World Cup. I was doing breakfast television. I was doing a weekly show for TV South in Southampton. To help keep all those balls in the air I had to keep away from drink as much as I could and, compared to the way I had been before and the way I would be again, I was very well-behaved. I regarded the flat in Chelsea as home, the first home I'd had for a long time, and I was doing nice, normal things like going to the theatre and the movies, reading, (especially biographies) and working hard. If Stavin thought she had it bad she should have asked Angie Best or Angie Lynn what the bad times can really be like.

Her public image was that of a Miss Goody Two Shoes of the butter-would-not-melt-in-her-mouth variety. But with me, at least, she wasn't like that at all. She used to ask me to squeeze her throat while we were making love. And she liked to go to sleep at night with something in her mouth; and it wasn't her thumb. She told everyone that she'd been a gymnast and that she was a fitness fanatic. She talked me into doing a keep-fit video record with her. I went along with her for my own purposes but it was a sham. In all the time I knew her I had never known her go near a gym or do any sort of exercise at all. I used to go out in the evening for a two- to three-mile run. She decided to come out with me one night. She got 50 yards down the road and started gasping for breath. And that was it – she went back to the flat and I never saw her running again.

161

Going through the motions of former Miss World, Mary Stavin's fitness fantasy. (© Brian Aris, Camera Press)

Then she said that what had really put the nail in the coffin of our relationship was when she had to fly back to Sweden for an operation and I hadn't gone with her. She said she thought she had cancer and there she was, poor girl, lying in bed crying her eyes out in the darkness, all alone and suffering and convinced she was dying. In fact I was working the day she flew out and couldn't cancel. And my understanding was that the operation was merely for a non-malignant cyst.

I find all these highly coloured stories about me hurtful. I've done stories myself but I've never sat down and told a load of nonsense. Yet every time anyone runs out of money I'm doused with another bucketful of abuse.

Stavin was at it again recently, reeling off the same old tales about drunken, unfaithful George Best. She has no right to keep trading off my name. We haven't been together for almost a decade. And what has she achieved since? I was sitting with Angie Lynn one night in her flat watching Stavin co-host the Miss World contest. Angie turned to me and said: 'I'm sorry for laughing, but this is the best comedy show I've ever seen.' Angie was right. Stavin was embarrassing. And this was the woman who was going to be a famous Hollywood movie star. But that's her problem. What I resent is the way she tries to embarrass me.

That's why I admire Angie Lynn so much. She's never spoken about our relationship and she certainly went through real hell with me. Angie got the real bad times. To call it a torrid relationship would be putting it mildly. I ended up getting banned from half the clubs in London, including Tramp. We had punch-ups and fights and if we put all the things together that we smashed up we'd be rich. Pictures, paintings, windows, everything got broken as we set about each other. And then we would go to bed and stay there for days.

Angie isn't a placid woman. She was also quite capable of doing her own walk-outs and that drove me crazy. She disappeared on me one New Year's Eve and didn't come back until the following day, insisting that she couldn't remember where she'd been. She went out in the middle of the night once, leaving me locked up in her flat. When she came back we would end up rolling on the floor trying to pull each other's hair out and screaming blue murder. Sometimes, when I was the worse for drink, she would bolt the door of her flat, leaving me ranting on the street outside. She often had to call the police to have them remove me. Once I punched my fist through her window and ended up walking home across London leaving a trail of blood behind me.

Even the lowest dives would go silent when we walked in. There is a club just off Regent Street which is open until seven o'clock in the morning. It is where the prostitutes, the pimps and the pushers hang out. I've never taken drugs. Not for any moral reason – remembering the problems that I had with drink, I'm hardly in a position to criticise other people's weaknesses – but because it just never appealed to me. A lot of people I've known have smoked pot and taken cocaine but I've always instinctively steered away from that. It doesn't appeal and I used to go crazy with Angie for hanging out in a club full of druggies. When I couldn't find her I would go there looking for her and if I found her we would start having a fight. The bouncers spent more time keeping an eye on me than they did on anyone else and in the end they barred me. Which takes some doing because the club was full of the scum of the earth.

With Angie Lynn, a moment of calm in our torrid relationship.
(© Dave Bennett)

And yet for all that I loved Angie, or came as close to love as I thought I could get. I was besotted by her; but in the end we had to break up – if we hadn't I quite seriously believe that one of us would have ended up killing the other. Angie has been offered a lot of money to write about our time together but she's always turned it down. I spoke to her about this recently and she said: 'George, if I ever need money that badly I will be in real trouble.' That's a very commendable, not to say unusual, attitude in this day and age and I can only applaud her for taking it. I am glad she hasn't been tempted. I'm tired of people making money out of me. And people have made a lot.

This isn't true of most of the men I played with or against back in the 1960s when we were riding the rainbow of fame and fortune. Ninety percent of the players who were around then are now forgotten men. Peter Storey went to jail for keeping a house of ill repute. Stan Bowles has a gambling problem. Then there's the tragedy of Jim Baxter.

Slim Jim was one of the greatest players ever to grace a football field. At his prime he was one of the most famous sporting names in the world. He was cool and arrogant, with control and balance, and who can forget the way, when he was playing for Scotland, he almost single-handedly demolished England's World Cup-winning side at Wembley? I bumped into Jim recently when I was in the North to appear on a television chat show. He had been brought along because the show's producers thought it would be nice if we met up again. The once slim Jim was now weighing in at around 20 stones. His clothes were old and frayed and he looked like the hard times he was living through. He didn't recognise me. Jim has had his problems and they've been similar to mine. Drink has obviously played its part, as it has with me. But if my problem remains a public one, his is, sadly, anonymous. I would rather be me.

Chapter Sixteen

Filthy Lucre

A T ITS PEAK my earning power was phenomenal. As long ago as 1969 I was making as much as £5,000 a week which, in those days, was a fortune. If I hadn't quit football I might now be worth anywhere between four and six million pounds. If I'd just looked after what I had I would be a millionaire. But as fast as the money rolled in, it rolled out again and I really don't have any clear idea where it all went. And we're talking about perhaps two or three million pounds in today's money that just mysteriously disappeared in a rush of good times and bad investments.

Di Stefano, the great Hungarian who played for Real Madrid, once said that I had to decide whether football was a business or a game. What Di Stefano didn't realise was that to me it was always a game and never a business. If it had been a business I would never have run away. I would have carried on playing and manipulated my career the way that players like Kevin Keegan did, and now I would be rich, the way he is.

But I didn't play the game that way. I just played the game and left the business side to other people and got ripped off right, left and centre. I don't complain about what happened. I don't even resent it. It was my fault, after all. It was just one of the unfortunate things that happen so often to footballers in Britain. It is almost as if the system was deliberately designed to ensure that you leave the game without any great fortune unless you happen to be either very lucky or very astute.

The clubs are dealing with boys with little education and no experience of the world. The lads are signed up at 13 or 14 and they are treated like kids for the whole time they're playing. I was a kid when I arrived at United. I was still a kid when I left. It's very easy to rip off a kid. At United everything was taken care of for me. My digs were paid for. The club took care of my hotel bookings and my airline tickets and my meals when we were away travelling. When I went abroad I was told to turn up, hand over my passport and get on the plane. When we got to wherever we were going a coach picked us up at the airport, took us to our hotel, drove us to the ground, picked us up after whatever match we were playing and then drove us back to the airport again. It was like one long school outing except that we didn't have to look at anything except the inside of a football stadium. We were certainly not expected to do any thinking for ourselves. And if you're not taught how to you don't. You can't. You don't have the experience of doing anything for yourself.

Then suddenly it's all over. The final whistle is blown and your career is at an end. You're on your own and you have to start taking care of yourself. That can be very difficult, no matter how intelligent or smart you may think you are.

I still find it difficult sometimes. I wouldn't know how to open a bank account. I wouldn't know how to go about getting a postal order because I've never had to do it. I wouldn't know how to send a registered letter, and the one time I went to the post office to buy a stamp I ended up at the wrong counter. I'm the product of a very long childhood.

Some players, of course, do manage to pick up the techniques of ordinary life. Many don't. Take Denis Law, for example. I invited him to join me recently on a coaching trip to Australia. He couldn't deal with the arrangements. He didn't know how to go about collecting his tickets or organising a visa and in the end he had to get my girlfriend, Mary Shatila, to do it for him. So did I. Paddy Crerand, another colleague from the glory days, came with me to Dubai to play in an exhibition game. Paddy, who played 16 times for Scotland, travels, for reasons best known to himself, on an Irish passport, which is a very Irish thing to do. He failed to get his passport stamped when he arrived. When he tried to fly out again a couple of days later he was detained at the airport by the authorities who said that because his passport wasn't stamped he couldn't possibly be in the country – and because he wasn't there he couldn't leave. He didn't know what was going on but then he wouldn't. Paddy was a footballer and footballers never have to deal with mundane problems like visas and entry permits. He was kept in Dubai until the matter was sorted out – by somebody else, of course.

Money is another aspect of the problem. The club may be

paying you very well but it doesn't provide you with the accountants or the lawyers to look after it for you. That's the one area where players are left to fend for themselves as best they can. That's why so many players, even ones who have enjoyed all the fame and financial rewards the game can give you, end up with very little at the end of it all. That's not the way it should be. I believe that the clubs have a responsibility to help their players look after their financial affairs. They should recommend decent, honest advisors instead of leaving them in the care of any Tom, Dick or Harry they might happen to meet in the bar one night. You only think about that in retrospect, of course. At the time you're too busy playing your football and enjoying your celebrity and spending your money. And, with my off-field income, I was earning more money than any player in this country had ever earned.

It all happened very quickly. At the age of 17 I was a young kid just breaking into the team and doing reasonably well. By the time I was 20 I was a superstar. In 1966, two months before my 20th birthday, I played for United against Benfica in Lisbon. It was a sensational game and we beat them, Eusebio and all, by the crushing margin of 5-1. Next day the headline in *Bola*, the leading sports paper in Portugal, read: 'Beatle called Best smashes Benfica.' I wasn't a footballer any more. I was a sporting pop star and I didn't know what was going on.

I had an agent by then, a man called Ken Stanley who had been introduced to me by Denis Law. Ken was all right. He worked hard and he didn't take a penny more than the 25 per cent commission we'd agreed on. But he didn't know, and I certainly didn't know, how massive the George Best industry was about to become; and we were overwhelmed by it. I started appearing in the pop magazines more than in the football ones. Girls screamed when they saw me and chased me down streets. I started receiving 10,000 fan letters a week and Stanley had to hire three girls full-time to answer my mail. A George Best fan club was started. I have a very heavy growth of beard and unless I shave twice a day I look unshaven. So I invented the original designer stubble, and guys were going away to try and cultivate what I was trying to get rid of.

With the fame came the money. I did commercials for everything; chewing gum, sausages, after shave, Spanish oranges, football boots. Despite the permanent five o'clock shadow one company paid me £20,000 to endorse their after shave and that just for an afternoon's work (the shoot was supposed to take all day but I went missing the night before and they didn't find me until lunchtime).

You could buy a house in Chelsea for £20,000 in those days. Que Sera, the dreadful futuristic house I built myself in Cheshire cost me £40,000. It was recently sold for over £1 million which gives an indication of how much I was earning back then. If I wanted a car I used to walk into the showroom and buy it with cash. I bought six E-type Jaguars in a row. I bought a Rolls Royce. If I wanted a glass of champagne I ordered a bottle of the best vintage. If I wanted to eat I went to the best restaurants. If I wanted a holiday I got on an aeroplane and went. And I still had more money left than I knew what to do with. Which was the trouble, because I really didn't know what to do with it.

I started investing in businesses I was advised to invest in. I became involved in half a dozen boutiques. I opened a travel agency. I opened a nightclub called Slack Alice. I found myself surrounded by advisors who would sit there and talk away amongst themselves about endowment policies and life policies and insurance policies. I didn't have a clue what it all meant but they carried on talking about me and what they were going to do with me as if I was not there. I might just as well have been invisible for all the attention they paid me. I was just a piece of high-priced meat. And when the meat started to go off these so-called advisors disappeared.

It would be fair to say, though, that I was not the easiest person to handle. And, in my naïvety, I enjoyed having people doing everything for me. I was only interested in playing football. Everything else was somewhere to go in the afternoons and the evenings. For in my mind the boutiques and the nightclubs were just hobbies. The trouble was that they started costing me a fortune. The travel business went out of business almost before it started. The idea was to fly prospective house buyers out to look at property in Spain and if they bought anything we were to get a percentage. No one ever bought anything. Slack Alice turned into a shambles. It made money initially but then we tried to expand. We opened a four-storey affair called Oscars. It might have worked except that first one partner sold out, then whoever they had sold to would sell out, and it ended in chaos with no one knowing who owned what.

By then the financial pipeline was starting to rust up. In 1971 I staged my first walk-out on United. In 1974 I walked out for the last time. I could still command a lot of money for playing and clubs like Stockport in the Fourth Division were prepared to offer me several hundred pounds a game because of the thousands of extra spectators I drew. But I had stopped doing commercial endorsements. Madame Tussauds melted down my waxworks. I wasn't exactly broke – I've never been broke except in the legal sense – but I was certainly no longer earning the sort of money I had been. That shouldn't have mattered. I had earned so much that I should have been set up for life. I was not. And I was still being taken advantage of.

For instance, when I came back from my first sojourn in America and signed for Fulham, part of the agreement was that they would put £10,000 down on an apartment for me. They did, and I took a place in Putney. When I decided to return to the U.S. I left instructions to sell the furniture and the hi-fi, put the flat on the market, and send me the £10,000. That was done and then I was told that the £10,000 had gone on expenses. I asked : 'What expenses?', and was told 'Phone calls, things like that.'

Who were they telephoning? The talking clock in Buenos Aires? But that's the way my luck goes.

I like to place an occasional bet on the horses and I used to use a bookmaker in Chelsea whom I would call once in a while. It was credit betting – a tenner here, £20 there. If I lost £20 you could be sure he would be looking for me in the pub the next day, waiting for me to come in so that he could collect. One day I won £180. Suddenly he was nowhere to be found, and I hear that he's in prison now.

Even when I did something which I thought was sensible it didn't work out the way it should have. Like when I put £27,000 into an Irish bank which, when it went bust, claimed that I owed it £8,000. The bank was based in Dublin and I was introduced to its Manchester branch by one of my partners in Slack Alice who had borrowed some money from it. I agreed to make a deposit of £27,000 of past earnings. The bank people told me that if I wanted to I could collect the interest once a week.

Now I may not be good at business but I can count. I was always good at Maths at school. It was my best subject. I could work out what the interest was on £27,000 and I never drew more than I was owed. Yet when the bank got into financial trouble they sent me a bill for the £11,000 I had drawn out which they claimed I owed them. There was no mention of the original £27,000 or the interest earned. Dumb I may be, but by my reckoning it owes me at least £16,000 plus interest.

That apart things did settle down a bit for me, financially, when I went to play in the United States in the mid '70s. I was well looked after and, for a while at least, I could push my financial cares to one side. The clubs there took care of my cars and accommodation. On top of that I was paid around £800 a week. Television and radio work was a bonus and added another few hundred dollars to the package. The sun shone and I was feeling quite happy with my two or three thousand dollars a week – which is more than many top First Division players earn in Britain today.

I was living on borrowed time, however. My footballing career in the United States was coming to an end. I decided that, for the sake of my health, it was time to leave California and return to Britain. When I did so in 1981 I walked straight into the tax problem that continues to dog me.

The Inland Revenue asked me for £16,000 in back tax on money earned when I was playing for Fulham. I was short of ready cash at the time so I offered them £10,000 right away with the remaining £6,000 to be paid within six months. They refused and demanded the full £16,000. It went on from there and I was declared bankrupt. The interest added up and by 1989 the amount due had come to around £40,000. I was denied a discharge because they said I had funds from my testimonial hidden away in Ireland.

I totally deny that I was trying to cheat or defraud the taxman. I have made safeguards for my son. I believe that it's my duty to do what I can for Calum and I made provision for him as I did when I put up half the money to buy his grandmother, Angela's mother, a house in Southend – and as

The good and the bad, but for once no bubbly. Myself with Ross Benson, my friend for 20 years. (© Terry O'Neil)

I did when I placed part of the receipts from my testimonial match in Belfast into a fund. But I certainly haven't been lining my own pocket. As far as I'm concerned I'm the one still owed money – especially by that bank in Ireland.

I'm no longer completely lost in this web of financial detail, however. I'm in my 40s and belatedly, I admit, I'm taking an interest in my financial affairs. And the more I look at them, the more convinced I am that the only person I can trust is myself. If I'd taken that approach 20 years ago I would now be a very rich man. Yet for all the upheavals and financial misfortunes I still consider myself lucky. I may have had my problems and I have certainly squandered a fortune in one bad investment after another. But I can still earn a living. The name George Best always earned more money off the field than it did on it, and while it obviously doesn't generate the income it once did, it still has earning potential.

Raich Carter, who played for the winning Arsenal side of the 1930s, once remarked: 'Old footballers should be shot.' They aren't, but it might be kinder if they were. When their professional usefulness is over they are told to pack their bags and go out and fend for themselves in a world that very few of them know how to deal with. A depressing number end up in prison, as compulsive gamblers, or in the gutter, reduced to living off what charity they can find. They are football's victims.

I may have lost a fortune but when I try I can at least still earn a living. And I'm grateful for that.

Chapter Seventeen

Being Best

I F I COULD change one thing, just one thing, just once in a while, it would be my face.

Now, after all this time, I can't help but wonder who this strange public person called George Best is. Is it me? Or is it some third person that people claim as their own, some two-dimensional cardboard cut-out who bears only a superficial resemblance to me, who doesn't belong to me but to anyone who chooses to claim it. It makes life difficult. Just getting out of bed can be a problem some days. Even taking my son to the zoo can degenerate into a dreadful hassle.

I took Calum there one bright Sunday afternoon. It should have been a wonderful afternoon out, the kind of afternoon every father should be able to enjoy. For me it was like running a gauntlet. As soon as we got there people surrounded us, taking our photographs, wanting autographs. They would stop me every few steps, asking me to pose for this and that, while all the time I was having to cope with buying the ice creams and making sure my son didn't run off. We were there for an ordinary afternoon out, the kind my own father used to take me on, and it turned from a zoo into a circus.

Back in the days when I was playing for Manchester United this attention never really bothered me, not at first. There were no problems then. I was always surrounded by people, by people I knew, and when an unpleasant situation happened to arise it tended to get defused by numbers. Not any more. Now, more likely than not, I am by myself or with just one other person. Now there is no one around to take the heat out of a situation. It is left to me and I am not always the best person to deal with the difficulties.

Most of the time, of course, it's all rather flattering. I haven't done anything of note in a footballing sense for close on a couple of decades now, yet people still remember me and that's very nice. I can get into a taxi and all the driver wants to talk about is how I was his hero when he was a kid, and how much pleasure I gave him (adding, all too often, that all the charisma and the great players have gone out of the game) and that is a hell of a compliment to be paid. They don't talk about Marjorie Wallace and they don't talk about me going to prison and they don't talk about the fights. It's the football, purely and simply the football. And they remember that I've remained a star, not because of all the aggravations and all the downs, but for what I did when I was playing. It's the same with Henry Cooper. When he walks down the street people stop him, and that's because of the boxing, something he did so well; and it's the same for me.

Unfortunately there's a downside, and it can be a very long way down. The days at the zoo ended with me finally deciding that I'd had enough. I rarely refuse a photograph or an autograph. Towards the end of the afternoon, however, a woman came up to me as I was walking along with Calum on my shoulders and asked me to sign a piece of paper. I replied, please, any other time, but I'm just here trying to have a good time with my son. She wasn't taking that for an answer, and the abuse started. She called me a flash bastard and a bighead and then, by way of an afterthought, the worst person in the world.

That sort of unseemly incident happens almost every day. No one ever picks a fight with Bobby Charlton but I can't walk down the King's Road in Chelsea without facing a torrent of invective. An old man sitting outside a pub might start slagging me off and saying what a waste of time I am and how I threw my life away. So what has he done to earn himself the right to criticise me? I try and laugh it off. At times that isn't so easy to do and when I get up in the morning and walk down the street to get myself some breakfast I never know which way the day is going to go.

It's weird, the reactions I provoke. Sometimes people give me the thumbs up. But when I see a group of men walking towards me it's always a toss up whether they're going to ask me for an autograph or smack me in the mouth; and it's been like that for 15 years now. It's like living in the twilight and sometimes it hurts. You only need one nutcase and you're in big trouble, and that trouble can be very painful indeed. You can end up with your skull cracked open.

That's what happened to me when I was going out with

Mary Stavin. We'd gone to the movies – I was stone cold sober, I hadn't had a single drink – and we came out at five minutes to eleven, five minutes before the pubs shut. We decided to pop into a pub called the Chequers in St. James's for one quick drink before it closed and then pick up a Chinese take-away on the way home.

There were four people in the place; two guys at the end of the bar who were discussing something loudly, and a young man and his girlfriend who were sitting on a bench by the stairs. I ordered a half of lager and Mary had an orange juice. I used the telephone to order the food we were going to pick up in ten minutes' time. And that was that – two people having a quick drink on the way home after a nice, pleasant evening at the pictures.

I was talking to the old man who ran the pub with his wife and I didn't take any notice of the man from the far end of the bar when he walked down towards me. He was holding a pint mug, one of those old pint mugs with a base about two inches thick. He came up behind me and he looked as if he was just about to finish his beer and leave. I carried on talking to the old man and Mary. Then he smashed the mug down on my head and split my skull.

I looked into the mirror behind the bar. I saw a fountain of blood coming out of my head. It was like a terrible dream. The young man who had been sitting with his girlfriend starting shouting, 'You bastard,' the old man I had been talking to was rushing around looking for a cloth with which to stem the blood. Mary panicked. She was screaming as she ran to the telephone to call the police and an ambulance.

I was slowly sagging to the floor and I nearly went down. But I wouldn't let myself go down. When I was playing I would never let one of the hard men employed to mark me know that he had hurt me. It was the same now. The next thing I remember, I had the man outside and I was going to kill him. I had him down in the gutter and I was banging his head on the road. An ambulance came and I remember hearing a young policewoman running down the street towards us and then dragging me off him. All the while the blood was pumping out of me. I had on a black leather jacket and it was completely covered with blood. The policewoman asked if there had been a fight or an argument and I replied that I didn't know the man, had never spoken a word to him; and they checked that with the people in the pub, who confirmed what I said.

They stuck me in the ambulance. But before they did I said to myself, you've got to have one more go at him. He was lying there in the street and I went over and kicked him between the legs and he must have lifted two feet into the air, with the poor policewoman saying, 'Oh, Mr Best, don't do that, please don't do that.' They took him away then and I went off in the ambulance to hospital. And as the ambulance men poked around in my hair, pulling out any little pieces of glass they could find, I'm thinking, 'This can't be true, this can't be true. I go to the movies and here I am in an ambulance, covered in blood, and worrying that the Chinese restaurant is going to be furious with me for not picking up the food I'd ordered.'

At the hospital they took all my clothes off and put them into a locker, sent Mary home, put me to bed and gave me a sedative to try and make me sleep. I couldn't. I kept asking myself, 'Why did that man do this to me?' Eventually, at around one-thirty, I decided I had had enough of looking at the ceiling. I got up and got dressed in my clothes which were soaked in blood. A poor little nurse came running up pleading, 'You can't leave, you musn't leave, let me get a doctor.' I told her that even if she did get a doctor it wouldn't make any difference because I was going home. I didn't. I went to Tramp – covered in blood, feeling terrible, too annoyed to sleep, confused, mentally out of it, thinking about Mary waiting at home, but too confused to care. Angie Best happened to be in Tramp when I walked in looking like a war victim, which is what I was, and she persuaded me to go to the police station to give a statement. I asked the desk sergeant if the man had said anything. The sergeant replied that he'd been in a bit of a state, what with one thing and another, and all they could make out was something about Liverpool, and that was all.

It turned out that he was a scaffolder and when he went to court he came up with a story about having problems at home. He got a three-month suspended sentence. When I was sentenced for drunken driving I got three months, unsuspended. Since I came out of prison I've had no trouble with the police. A few days after his court case the man who had cut my skull open with a beer mug went into another pub and did the same thing to someone else. There were people quite prepared to enforce a harsher sentence on the guy. A few days after the court case I was walking down Jermyn Street, just around the corner from the pub, a young man came running after me and said that the man who had attacked me was working on a construction site nearby and did I want him to throw him off. I got a lot of calls from Belfast from people offering to 'take care of the guy', as they put it. But that's not the way things can be done. It's not the way I believe things should be done. In this life you have to deal with your own problems and my problem is being who I am; or, more complexly, what people think I am.

I was never a hard man on the field, but because of how I played and what I have done since I stopped playing I generate a hostile reaction in a lot of people. Perhaps it's jealousy on their part. Perhaps they want to prove that they are better than me. It may even be partly my own fault. I don't go looking for trouble, but nor will I cross the street for anybody. Why should I? I've done nothing to be ashamed of. I'm no worse than anyone else. On the contrary – I've actually done certain things better than anyone. And if people really want to take issue with me about something, so be it. Someone once said to me, 'You're either very brave or very crazy', and it might just be that I am both. But it can put a dampener on your day. It's not the nice people I mind. But there always seems to be someone waiting – in a bar, in a restaurant – who after a few drinks thinks he owns you and starts pushing you and pulling you and insulting you.

It's not just the yobs, either, who want to prove to you just how tough they are. I don't go into places that have a reputation for trouble, but then I don't have to to find it. There's an Indian restaurant in the Fulham Road in Chelsea. It's a smart place full of smart, respectable people and I went in there with Angie Lynn one night. It was the same story. I was sober, we'd been to the movies, which I love (my favourite films, by the way, include *Charlie Bubbles*, *The Deer Hunter*, *My Left Foot* and *Mona Lisa*). We stopped off on the way home for a meal. There were six businessmen in suits sitting at a table nearby. One of them stood up and came over and said that he was going to tell me one or two things about myself – about how I'd gone wrong, and what a fool I'd been. I told him that I wasn't interested in listening to what he thought he had to say; that I was having a quiet dinner with my girlfriend and for him to leave us alone.

He wasn't having any of that. He told me that I needed someone to speak to. I replied that even if I did – and I didn't – it wouldn't be him. I told him again to go away, more forcefully this time. By now Angie was hanging on to my leg. She knew what I was like in situations like this: sooner or later I snap. In the end I told him that if he didn't go back and join his friends I would smack him in the mouth. It was all very unpleasant and degrading and in the end, quite humiliating. Suddenly a nice, quiet meal had become a confrontation. It didn't end with blows being exchanged. It didn't have to. The damage had been done; another evening had been ruined.

There are always people who go to bars looking for excitement. There are always people who, after a couple of pints, turn into fighting drunks, and the combination of drink and spotting me can sometimes prove just a little too much, especially if they happen to be in a group and want to prove that they are Jack the Lads. Before, when I was younger and still playing top-class football, I would walk away from that kind of situation. But then I got to a stage where I decided that I'd had enough, that if I wanted to sit in a corner by myself and have a drink I would do so and that if someone wanted to be rude I would be rude back. I certainly wouldn't punch anyone without reason. But if someone comes up and threatens me or tries to hit me then I'm not going to stand there and bother to try and talk him out of it any more. I decided, without thinking about it or analysing it, that I'd had enough.

That really doesn't mean that I court these situations. I don't. I will avoid them when I can. I would have liked to have seen Eire play Northern Ireland in the World Cup qualifying match in 1989. Paddy Crerand, my colleague from my Manchester United playing days, invited me to go with him to the game. I declined.

'Don't be stupid, people are different in Ireland,' Paddy kept saying. 'They won't bother you.' They don't bother Paddy but with all the respect in the world, Paddy isn't me. I told him: 'Paddy, this is Ireland and Eire have got a chance of going to the World Cup finals the first time ever if they beat Northern Ireland. You think I'm not going to be bothered?'

It would have been bad before the game. It would have been terrible after the game, especially if Northern Ireland had won rather than lost. And heaven knows what it would have been like throughout the match. So I decided against. Not because I was frightened but because when you weigh everything up, a football game is supposed to be an enjoyable entertainment – and unless you happen to be a masochist there is very little enjoyment to be had in enduring ninety minutes of personal abuse, which is what I would have faced. So, instead, I watched the game on television in the safety and comfort of a hotel room near Dublin airport.

There is, as I've said, the upside to being who I am – and in being remembered for what I did. I enjoy flying first-class. I appreciate the notoriety that allows me to continue earning a very decent living. I love driving around in limousines. I like being invited to premières and saying hello to Dustin Hoffman. And in an obvious way, I enjoy the adulation. It's just the flip side of the coin that is so difficult to deal with.

Some years ago I went to Japan on a charity tour and the biggest names in football were there – Pele, Paolo Rossi, Kevin Keegan. We were in the hotel lobby and the only person the Japanese were really interested in was me. The others were asked for one or two autographs; I had 40 or 50 people lining up in front of me. That was very pleasing. But if that's one difference between myself and the others, there is another – which is that nobody wants to go up to Franz Beckenbauer or Pele or Eusebio or Johann Cruyff and smack them in the mouth. For me just to go out for a cup of coffee entails a risk; and this constant threat terrifies any woman I happen to be with.

But I suppose these difficulties make me appreciate the good things so much. I figure that because of all the aggravation I find myself subjected to I'm entitled to my perks. At the same time, however, it can be, if not exactly frightening, then certainly very depressing. I wake up sometimes and think, another walk down the King's Road into this weird twilight zone of confrontation, another day sitting with my back to the wall waiting for trouble to come busting through the bar door. And I sometimes wonder if this is why I started drinking: to try and pretend that I'm not where I am. It's not an excuse, but it's certainly a fact that when I'm drinking I can put everything away onto the backburner.

I can understand why some famous people become reclusive. You may laugh at them but I often think to myself, 'Where can I go?' The trouble is that I can't go anywhere except where I am. I couldn't move to a desert and cut myself off. I earn my living out of football and I have to be where football is played; and that's not on a remote mountain top somewhere but in cities like London and Manchester. There is, of course, a disassociation in all this, and sometimes when I think about myself and the way my life has turned out it is as if I am considering a different person.

Yet for all the problems I wouldn't change my life. I walk down the streets and I look at the men working on building sites and coming in and out of offices and sitting in traffic jams and I think, 'I've never been through that.' I've never had to put up with the drudgery that most people have to live through. I think, 'You've crammed more into your life than they have. You've had more fun and more excitement. You've never had to do the same thing year in, year out.' And for that, at least, I can be thankful.

There's still always the thought, though: 'How would it be if I wasn't me?'

If my life has had its down side it has also had its glorious, delicious highs. And the past nine years, apart from the bad spells with the booze, have been tremendous. I've worked for ITV on two World Cups, TV AM for almost a year, and done a season for TV South (now Southern TV). I've travelled a lot – to the Middle and Far East, to America and Australia and all across Europe, sometimes coaching, sometimes playing in exhibition matches, always travelling first-class. One day I might be lunching with the Prime Minister at 10 Downing Street or sitting next to the ruler of somewhere like Dubai and being treated like royalty. The next I will be in a pub having a drink with a few mates – ordinary hard-working men who work in offices and storerooms – and I enjoy the contrast.

It makes me laugh to read those same old stories about George Best, fallen superstar, the great soccer idol who threw it all away – written by men who barely earn in a year what I can still earn in a fortnight. I'm not like Jim Baxter or Peter Storey. My future is in my own hands and I can do with it what I want – and that's a marvellous privilege in a world where more and more you seem to have to do what other people tell you. I've eaten suckling pig under a clear, starlit sky in Acapulco. I've sailed across the magnificent Sydney Harbour. I've dined on oysters and champagne in Surfer's Paradise in Australia. I've drunk the finest wines and made love to the most beautiful women. There are still moments when the drink gets on top of me but they are not nearly as frequent as they used to be, and sometimes my alleged bad behaviour is really just a case of give a dog a bad name. My recent trip to Australia is an example of that.

I went there, supposedly with all expenses paid, to do some coaching and appear in a few charity matches. Denis Law went with me and we did what was required of us. When we got to Tasmania, however, the organiser told us he had no money. When we got to Sydney things got worse. We were shown an itinerary which said that we had a kick-about game with some local businessmen at two-thirty in the afternoon and an 'optional' coaching session an hour and a half's drive away which was supposed to last from nine-thirty in the morning until four-thirty in the afternoon. We said that it was impossible to do both, that we couldn't be in two places at the same time, but as it was 'optional' it wasn't a problem. But it was, because the optional coaching engagement wasn't optional at all – the organiser, Billy Millen, had signed a contract on our behalf two months earlier.

I got angry. Denis got angry – and Denis very rarely gets angry with anyone. I got angrier when I discovered that the organiser's friends were having dinner at our hotel – and sticking their bill on my account. Then the hotel presented us with bills to pay because the organiser had now disappeared off to Melbourne. The hotel contacted him there and he told them to send it off, that he would pay it, but by then we had had enough. We decided to cut our losses and fly off to Los Angeles for a few days' holiday. By now, of course, Millen is having to answer press enquiries about what's going on. He has to say something and it's very easy to wheel out the old, 'Oh, George is drunk' excuse. But I wasn't drunk

– if I had been why have I been invited back to Australia again?

It's the perfect way for someone to get themselves off the hook, though, because everyone knows I drink. But not the way I used to. The demons are not raging as they once did. My life is coming back under control; and Mary Shatila has been a big reason why.

We got together three years ago, and apart from being my girlfriend she is also my friend. She has helped me sort out my business affairs and for a while she almost took over my life, arranging things and getting me organised. It is a cliché to say that she's put me on the straight and narrow – if that wasn't where I wanted to be no one could have got me there – but she's certainly steered me in the right direction. She's been good for me. And now that she has a lot of problems of her own, in some ways our roles are reversed. She has a daughter from her marriage to a Lebanese and he's absconded with the child who is now somewhere in Beirut. Mary has not seen her for a year now and that is a terrible hurt to bear. It really gets to her at times. I can relate to that because of Calum. But at least I know where he is and at least I can see him. Mary doesn't even know for sure where her child is. I'm as supportive as I can be. I tell her that it will work out, and that we have to really believe that it will.

We have our disagreements, of course, and we've had a couple of very heated exchanges, but only for one reason – because of the situation involving her daughter. She's a wonderful lady. The idea of George Best living a life of cosy domesticity may be an unusual one, but we really are very happy together. I can still look back on the old days and smile at the memories, but I'm also very pleased with the way my life is going now.

If there's one thing still lacking it's the buzz I used to get from appearing in front of a huge football crowd. Nothing has ever hit that height and probably never will. But that's a problem that applies to all top athletes, and as I get older I'm finding it easier to come to terms with, thank goodness. And I can take consolation in the fact that I played football when it really was a glorious game.

When I played you didn't complain if you were hurt in a tackle. You didn't rush to the newspapers if you had a

Mary Shatila; my lover, my friend and my strength. (© Terry O'Neil)

disagreement with your manager. There was loyalty; players didn't shuffle around from club to club the way they do now. There was also grace and good manners in the game. When I was in Dubai to see Liverpool play Celtic I was appalled at the way Kenny Dalglish, the manager of the most successful club side in Britain, took the mickey out of a waiter because he didn't happen to speak English. We liked a good time too – but it never included anything like that.

I find these changes sad and today I enjoy watching Rugby

League, Rugby Union and American football as much as I do soccer, which is something that, 20 years ago, I would never have thought of saying. They play like men, and they act like men.

I'm still optimistic about football, however. There's an old saying that the ball is round and that it is made round to go round; and there are signs of better things to come. For one thing, there are some excellent young players coming up. Marco Gabbiadini at Sunderland is an exceptionally exciting prospect. I went to watch him play against Fulham and even though he was not 100 percent fit he looked in a class by himself. His sharpness was rewarded by two goals. His reflexes in front of goal remind me of Gerd Muller, the great West German striker – and he has more skill on the ball than Muller ever did, which is about as complimentary as I can get.

Tony Daly at Aston Villa is another player I will pay to watch. He has pace and skill and he scores goals. His daft haircut gives him character and I love characters in football. I look forward to seeing him, which is a rare thing for me to say. You feel that buzz when he gets the ball. You expect something to happen and nine times out of ten it does. If he has one fault it's his final ball, but that will come with experience. Rodney Wallace and Matthew Le Tissier also generate that buzz. They are sharp, they have touch and speed off the mark and they score goals which is, after all what you pay for. It's players like these, Paul Gascoigne, QPR's Andy Sinton and Chelsea back Tony Dorigo who hold the key to the future. If they continue to develop there's no limit to what they can achieve. They play the game the way I believe it should be played – with flair, style and individuality.

That's the way I played football, and I played the game when it was fun and free and the crowds roared with pleasure, not hate. I scored goals that people still cherish in their memories and tell their children about. If football is an art I was an artist, and I'm proud of that. I won two League championship medals and I took Manchester United to victory in the European Cup.

When I was a little boy growing up on the Cregagh estate in Belfast I wanted to be a footballer more than anything else. Years later, Pele called me the greatest footballer in the world. That is the ultimate salute to my life.

Donation